Uncoverings 1984

Volume 5 of
the research papers of
American Quilt Study Group

Edited by Sally Garoutte

Title calligraphy: Linda MacDonald

Published by the American Quilt Study Group
105 Molino avenue, Mill Valley, CA 94941
Manufactured in the United States

ISBN 0-9606590-4-8
ISSN 0277-0628

Library of Congress catalogue card number: 81-649486

CONTENTS

Introduction

Sandra Metzler

Researchers of American quiltmaking history often begin their long search for information with the profound inspiration of only a single quilt, a panel of quilted petticoat, a faded pinky-brown fabric scrap or a brittle hand-scrawled note with one unknown woman's retrospections of her life and her art. Something tangible that somehow speaks to the quilt historian spurs that person's curiosity for understanding of the times and of themselves, even if it takes a lifetime of questioning. Since 1980, the American Quilt Study Group has taken great pride in supporting through publication quilt researchers and their invaluable work, with the satisfaction that each year's *Uncoverings* will add more significant pieces to the greater body of women's history.

Depending upon the original inspiration, American quiltmaking traditions are approached by researchers from a valid variety of ways, but ever cognizant of the importance of the "quilt context." As one reads through the studies herewith, one senses the "assemblage" of social, cultural and temporal factors at play on the maker and object. Virginia Gunn's essay, for example, illustrates how Crazy quilts and Outline quilts were the popular responses by needleworkers to the decorative art/art needlework movement of the late nineteenth century. Focusing on one family and their quilts in a specific region over several generations, however, is the subject of Sandra Todaro's research. Narrowing even further, Nancilu Burdick examines through primary sources one specific quiltmaker, Talula Bottoms, and her life's work of over one hundred quilts — a felicitous and excellent example of documentation.

Still in light of the social context of the times, Tandy Hersh searches for eighteenth century quilted petticoats in her study while also raising the issue of skilled needlewoman or professional as maker. Fundraising quilts by "anonymous" women and their social need and existence through time is presented by Dorothy Cozart, and Merikay Waldvogel studies the WPA Milwaukee Handicraft Project and the quilts produced during times of hardship. In a broader approach, James Liles discusses the textile dyes available to quiltmakers throughout time, suggesting how those dyes may have influenced the products preserved today.

Louise Townsend's comprehensive survey of quilt patterns appearing in the *Kansas City Star* newspapers will help define "Midwest" quilts as a cultural region with its own quilt history assemblage. Indeed, perhaps some of the most exciting research results now being discovered are these regional overviews. Missouri-German quilts, for instance, are shown by Suellen Meyer to be reflective of the people and their culture in all physical respects. In addition, quilts of South Carolina have been grouped by several distinct cultural and geographical regions by researcher Laurel Horton: the Piedmont, the Sandhills, the Coastal Plains and the Sea Islands.

Thus, with the cumulative results of these studies and others year after year, we will piece together the fascinating regional quiltmaking traditions of America. It is the hope of the American Quilt Study Group that the readers of *Uncoverings* will enjoy and cherish their heritage and perhaps themselves be sparked to seek out some of the many other unanswered questions in the history of American quiltmaking and the people who made them.

Talula Gilbert Bottoms and her Quilts

Nancilu B. Burdick

Two quilts made just 50 years apart (1885 and 1935), a little book of memories written at age 81, and several boxes of old letters were the materials at the root of this research on my grandmother's quilts. But it was an unplanned visit to the Folk Art Center of the Southern Highland Handicraft Guild in North Carolina, resulting in encouragement by Bets Ramsey and Sally Garoutte, that made me aware of Talula as a quilter whose story should be told. The two quilts, the Feather and the Lifeboat, then seemed like parentheses enclosing her lifetime of quilting, just waiting for someone to discover the history between them. Yet evidence from the above materials and from personal interviews, photographs, and letters from the present owners, shows that numerous quilts were made after 1935, and that there are yet more to discover.

Talula Bottoms (1862–1946) was a delicate little woman who bore 12 children and raised nine of them and three orphan children to adulthood, while doing the work of a Southern farmer's wife without indoor plumbing or other modern conveniences until she was 78 years old. During this time she pieced as many as 200 quilts and quilted most of them herself. She continued to piece quilt tops after the old home was remodeled to accommodate her son's family (leaving no room for her quilting frame) and ceased her beloved work only a few weeks before her death at age eighty-four. I have been able to verify over 100 existing quilts made by her, more than forty of which I have seen and photographed.

She was born on February 15, 1862, about 20 miles from Atlanta, Georgia, at a time when the South was still hopeful of victory in the Civil War. Atlanta was the chief depot for Confederate military supplies and was therefore a prime target for General Sherman in his

Nancilu B. Burdick: 35 Countryside Lane #8, Orchard Park, NY 14127

march to the sea. Yet the war seemed far away as John Joseph Gilbert and his wife Holly welcomed their second daughter and fourth child into their comfortable Fayette County farm home. It was not until the guns could be heard as Sherman's men approached Atlanta in the summer of 1864 that John Gilbert knew he must take his children and Holly—expecting another child in December—to a safer place in south Georgia. They would return in November, just a few weeks before baby Minta was born, and after the destruction of Atlanta, to find Fayette County devastated but their home still intact.

One of Talula's earliest memories is of that return home by wagon when the children, black and white together, were allowed to eat bread soaked in molasses spilled in the wagon from a broken jug. The ravages of the war and its aftermath included the death of Holly Gilbert a year later when Talula was not yet four years old. Her mother's funeral was on Christmas Eve, 1865, and seven months later her father brought home a new wife. Talula had been told that her father would bring her "Ma" home that day; the disappointment at not seeing her own mother so disturbed her that for months afterwards when she would be out in the yard playing, she "would go sit on a certain stump that was there and cry for a long time each day, and no one could get me to tell what I was crying about."[1]

After the war economic conditions were so harsh the children had to pick up the work (formerly done by slaves) as soon as they were able to hold a broom or wring the heavy work-clothes, sheets, and even quilts, out of the steaming wash water. For Talula this was at age ten; after her older sister was married she would often have to stay out of school to help.

> When we would do the washing, my step-mother put turpentine in the little jar of lye soap we had to use to wash; and washing the clothes in warm water with our hands (for no washboards or machines were known in Georgia at that Time) we both took a bad case of rheumatism ... from breathing the fumes. I had to crawl to the fireplace every morning when I'd get up, and rub my feet and ankles to get them so I could hobble about. Little sister Minta was in bed flat of her back and couldn't get up at all.... I never got the

Fig. 1. Talula Gilbert at age 16 (copied from an old tintype).

(pain and swelling) out of my ankles until after I was married and got rested being off my feet. I had to be on them so much that they could not get well.

Part of that time I couldn't do one thing to be on my feet, so my step-mother had me card bats for quilting quilts. I carded a hamper basket piling full besides some more for one quilt. I don't know how many quilts that one big basket full made, tho guess there was enough for several quilts.[2]

Soon there were four more children in the family, making ten, plus hired men who were boarders, for whom to wash, iron, cook, clean, spin and weave, knit and sew, make a garden year-'round, milk the cows, and raise the chickens. No wonder Talula had not been taught to sew, for her step-mother Ann Eliza was a meticulous, practical woman, and Talula was now her chief help. Yet even at age ten Talula had seen the beautiful quilts her own mother had made, and no amount of discouragement or harsh circumstances could prevent the eventual flowering of her talent.

I would find needles and pins on the floor where they had

dropped them when at work and I would save them to sew
and pin my doll clothes ... I kept them in the loft of our
playhouse. My Father had built a small house at the well to
keep the milk cool, but my stepmother did not use it, so the
two little girls had it for a playhouse. I was large enough to
work ... but kept my dolls and sewing things there. One
day I had stayed up in the loft so long and neglected my
work, that my stepmother said she would have my brother
go up there and throw them down (in the lot, where the
stock would trample them). I began to cry and told her I
wanted to save my needles and pins and quilt scraps. She
told me to go up and get them then. So I saved (them) and
began to piece on a quilt.

My girl friend gave me a little square she had made and
told me to make a square for her. So I pretended to make
one, but alas, it was crank-sided; some pieces were larger
than others and it was a mess, for I had never been taught
to sew anything. Tho I gave it to my friend, as it was the
best I could do. It was a nine patch square....

Then I went to work to make a quilt like the square the
girl gave me ... when I was thru my other work of cooking,
washing, etc., I'd piece on my quilt squares when I could,
but they were kindly like the first square, tho I got enough
squares to make a quilt. Then my grandmother helped me
put it together.[3]

Though the girl children did not work in the fields, they had to
help with the ginning by driving the horses to turn the big cog
wheel, by dragging the huge hampers of cotton, into which the
pickers had emptied their sacks, up to the gin, and by pulling the
"lint cotton" hampers up to the press. Then after the day's work was
over, it was the children's job to clean the lint room:

In those days there would be a lot of the fine cotton that
would stick around and up in the roof of the lint room. My
stepmother would have that saved to quilt the common
everyday quilts with, tho it would be so dusty and dirty
we'd have to put it on the bed scaffold and whip the dust
and dirt out of it. Then we'd have to card it into bats with
an old-fashioned pair of cards. Then we'd lay every bat, one
by one on the lining of the quilt to be quilted which was already laced into the frames. Then the quilt top was put on

and sewed down around the edge of the lining. Then the everyday, or night quilts were laid off in shells to be quilted.

The nice quilts, as they called them, were quilted by the piece and were nicely quilted.[4]

Ann Eliza's exacting standards and Talula's desire to please her combined to keep her a veritable slave to the family all through her teen years. Her sisters and her brother's wife urged her to marry any one of the many eligible young men who were, one after the other, her "beaux." Her stepmother highly disapproved of the only one she liked, young Tom Bottoms, whose widowed mother was struggling to hold on to the family farm. Tom, born in 1860, had been his father's 17th child and his own mother's eighth, and had reached manhood just at the time the depression following the Civil War was severely undercutting the gains the Southern people had made after Reconstruction. Tom lived with his mother, Eliza McElroy Bottoms, in the old home his father had built in the 1840's, and he was her only support.

The reason Talula's family gave for disapproval of Tom was that he had "no business sense." More important perhaps was a not-so-subtle social distinction: the Bottoms women had to work in the field and the Gilbert women did not. But Talula persisted in allowing Tom to come to see her, for in her character was a stubborn strength born out of her early hardships, and a sure knowledge of what she wanted. (Figure 1) Early in her memoir she wrote:

When I grew up I had lots of beaux but didn't like them until once a young fellow with black hair and black eyes came to see me, shyly. I had liked him since childhood and one Sunday while riding with Tom Hill just after he had asked me to marry him, we met the blackheaded boy riding a pony. Right then and there I decided I'd never marry any-one as long as he was single, tho I didn't know he'd ever come to see me, or want me to marry him.[5]

Yet for nearly two years after Tom's proposal, Talula would not give him a firm answer. She explains her uncertainty:

It was hard for me to decide what to do … as I had been told by my step-mother that if I married I would take con-sumption and die like my mother and my aunt did … I was a weakly little girl … and I got stronger, and have lived with the one I liked best to be 81 years old, and hope I can live with him longer.[6]

When Tom's visits abruptly stopped (he had split his foot open with an axe, could not walk, and was ashamed for her to know it), and she did not hear from him for several months, Talula grew alarmed. She broke with tradition, quite improperly wrote him a note, and the wedding took place ten days later. It is revealing that not until after her marriage was Talula able to piece and applique "the nice quilts, as they called them" or to be free of the rheumatic pain and swelling in her ankles and feet.

> When I got married, I had quilted only one quilt and had one top ready to quilt, that I had pieced at nights and little odd times. I had always had so much work to do for the family that I had no time for piecing quilts ... I loved to piece and work on my quilt work, so I decided to put in every moment of my time that I was not busy at something that was needed more, I'd work on my quilt work ... When I could get the material to work with.[7]

Within weeks after her marriage, Talula found out her mother-in-law was in imminent danger of losing her farm. She had signed notes that had essentially mortgaged the place to cover losses by an older son in his saw-mill business. The debts, though small by today's standards, could not be paid, without "stinting to the bone." There was talk of letting Mr. Blalock, who had bought up the notes, have the place and the family moving as homesteaders to Sand Mountain, Alabama, where "people could inter [sic] a place by paying $18 for an intery of 160 acres with sometimes a small house and a few acres cleared."[8] One of Tom's older brothers had already moved there. Talula was heartsick. Finally she decided to tell her father, who soon paid off the notes, took the farm and deeded it to Talula. The humiliation was hard on Tom, but the improved conditions enabled Eliza Bottoms, a fine quilter in her own right, and Talula to buy new material for quilts.

> I would get patterns from anyone I could. I even borrowed one quilt from my step-mother's sister ... It was very pretty. Then I got the patterns off all my own mother's nice quilts, and one off my step-mother's nice quilt. She didn't have but one, that was the Orange Bud. But my grandmother Gilbert told me lots of times that it was my own mother's quilt....[9]

The nice quilts that Talula tells of having made during the first

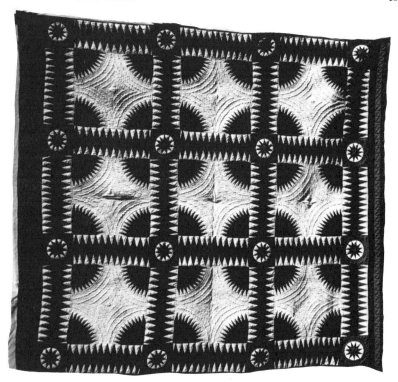

Fig. 2. Rocky Mountain, pieced 1884, quilted 1893. Photo courtesy Mary Alice Butler.

years of her marriage are ones she herself considered special. The ones she names in her letters and her memoirs from this period besides the Orange Bud are the Road to Texas, Feather, Rocky Mountain, Basket of Flowers, Basket of Pears, Magnolia Leaf, Star and Chain, and Glittering Star. Of these, six have been found and two others are thought to be packed away in trunks or boxes in storage rooms, too difficult for the families who have them to get at in their present circumstances.

The Rocky Mountain (Figure 2), probably Talula's first nice pieced quilt, was made, as were all of these early quilts, from patterns she cut herself by borrowing quilts she admired. This one came from her step-mother's sister, Molly Tarpley, later to be her father's third wife. The Tarpleys had come to Fayette County from

Henry County, and no doubt the quilt's name was the one this pattern was known by in Georgia at that time, although most authorities today call it New York Beauty.

Talula's Rocky Mountain, pieced before 1885 and quilted in 1893, is a striking red, green, and white quilt, each tiny red triangle cut by hand and joined to quarter circles of green against white to form the 16-inch blocks. The 7-inch wide sash joining the blocks is pieced with red and white triangles on center strips of green. The points on the sash where the blocks meet and the four corners are emphasized by 7-inch squares of red into which are pieced small red, green, and white sunbursts. Three 1½-inch borders of green, red, green at top and bottom make the quilt's size 76 x 85 inches. The entire top is made by hand with the tiniest of stitches and the quilting is exquisite, creating an overall spectacular effect. The only machine stitching on the quilt joins the pieces of coarsely woven unbleached muslin lining and attaches the red binding. The quilting was done by eye measurement following the design of the quilt; no marking is visible and the quilt has never been cleaned or washed.

The Basket of Pears, called Pear Basket by Talula's granddaughter in Nevada who inherited it through her father Matt, is an unusual quilt. Its stylized baskets with pieced saw-tooth handles contain one pear and two leaves. The same tiny calico prints, one yellow on green, the other white and green on red that are pieced with white muslin to form the blocks, are also used for the wide red, green, red sash that joins them, and for the three borders. The quilt has an interesting composition in that the fifteen full blocks, set diagonally so the basket handles face the center, come out uneven, and the bottom corners are completed with quarter squares, with nine triangle half-squares showing basket handles and pears around sides and top of quilt, and two at the bottom. With its fine grid quilting, the quilt has a subdued old look showing it has no doubt been put on the best bed for company over the years. It is now with Talula's great-grandson's family in Texas, who also have the Star and Chain.

The Magnolia Leaf was apparently the local name of a variation of an old pattern identified as Oak Leaf and Reel in *America's Quilts and Coverlets*.[10] Talula's leaf, appliqued in dark green calico is slightly wider than those in the quilt pictured in Safford and Bishop's book; the little "acorns" are more rounded, and the square in the center is the same dark green calico as the leaves so that the magnolia leaf seems to be laid over the red print reel. This is the only one of

Fig. 3. The Feather, appliqued 1885, quilted 1892.

Talula's quilts so far discovered adorned with hearts in the quilting. It is now displaying its ancient beauty for Talula's great-grand-daughter in Ohio, who also has another striking old quilt, intricately pieced by Talula in yellow and red on white muslin in a pattern today known as Chinese Fan.[11]

Talula's daughter Mollie Ruth considered the Feather (Figure 3) the most exceptional of all her mother's quilts. When some time after 1915 she and her older sister Almira "drew straws" for this quilt and the Rocky Mountain, Mollie Ruth did not draw the one she wanted, nor did Almira. Yet each could see the other's disappointment, so after some hesitation the exchange was made. Both quilts ended up with Almira when Mollie Ruth predeceased her in 1978, but Mollie Ruth had already had more than thirty years to enjoy it.

The story of the Feather is best told in Talula's own words:

Dear Daughter,

Yes! I just got your letter ... felt sure of one telling that
you got the quilt. Glad it went thru all right. Glad you had
it sent to you. Know you enjoy showing it. I got the pattern
from "Sister Sousan" Bro. George's wife. She made two of
them, one for Papa's mother and one for herself.

When Mother [Eliza Bottoms] divided her quilts, Mrs.
Liza Elmore was there and all the daughter-in-law(s). So
Mrs. Liza placed the quilts on five chairs, as Mother had 5
children ... We in-laws all went into the hall, and Mrs. Liza
fixed them as she pleased ... She placed the Feather quilt on
first chair, also other best ones, and then the second best on
second chair, and the next best on next, and so on, until the
worst ones were on the fifth chair. So naturally, the oldest
one was the one who got the first chair (and the best quilts),
next oldest got next best, and so on. So Sister Sousan got
the Feather quilt ... Then after all was over and the others
had carried their quilts away, Mother said to me that she
"did want Tommie to have the Feather quilt" ... So
Tommie got the poorest bunch; they were all very good, but
just very common quilts.

Well, I decided I'd get the Feather pattern and make myself one. So I soon got the pattern and goods, and made it
when I was about 23 or 24 years old. Then I kept it with
several other nice tops I had made ... as we were married
three years before any children came. So I made nice quilt
tops during that time. After the children began to appear
(there was one each year for 5 or 6 years, and I had my
hands full) the nice pretty tops had to lay away in a trunk
until I could have a little time to quilt them ... when I
quilted the Feather quilt I had 3 little boys and they liked to
play in the yard. But it was funny to them for one at a time
to come in and stand by me while I quilted and fan me with
a large palmetto fan. When one was tired I had him go out
and let another come in to fan me. Now this is the history
of the Feather quilt.[12]

Talula's Feather, circa 1885, is appliqued in olive green (somewhat
changed from its original color) and bright red on fine white muslin,
with a coarsely-woven unbleached muslin lining. The batting is a

thin layer of hand carded cotton and the quilting is done in exquisite scallops, tiny even stitches 10 or more per inch, to follow the pattern of the plumes. The appliqued plumes, eight to each square, four pairs of red and green turned toward each other, are quilted so as to leave a small plume-shaped puff in the center of each one. There are nine blocks, the three center ones being 27½ inches square and the six end ones 27½ x 30 inches, making the overall size 82 by 87 inches. The quilt is alive with color, texture and movement. Its only flaw is that it is machine bound, rather unevenly, as if Talula was just learning to do that kind of sewing machine work.[13]

It is difficult to guess whether this was the Feather variation of any particular family, for as Talula says, she borrowed quilts from anyone she could. And though Susan Collins Bottoms was the source of Talula's pattern in 1885, it would be impossible to say where Susan's came from. Found among Talula's old quilt patterns was a single brittle sheet, the cover page of a 1928 *Southern Agriculturist*; reversed it shows a picture of a Prince's Feather block, and describes another old Feather quilt found in a remote country home in Alabama.[14]

Talula's letter to Mollie Ruth continues:

I had made 5 or 6 real nice pretty quilt tops before any children came to our home ... After several years of regular work with the children I began to quilt the nice quilts ... the Feather first. So I finally got them all quilted ... Then as they married, I gave a nice quilt to each. Ary got the Basket of Flowers, Matt got Basket of Pears, Emmett got Magnolia Leaf, Roger got The Road to Texas, I think. Then came the division of the Feather and Rocky Mountain quilts, so you and Sister got them. Burlie got the Glittering Star, I think, Gilbert is to get the Star and Chain quilt. It isn't as pretty as the others, though I may make them a prettier one, but can't quilt it now.[15]

The Glittering Star that Talula mistakenly thought Burlie got has been found in a cedar chest in Alabama, waiting for the return from the mission field in Africa of Almira's youngest daughter. Each star of the 30 12-inch blocks is pieced with 3 to 15 different calicos. Each of the 8 diamonds that make up the stars contain three calico and two muslin pieces so that the calico points are set apart to give the glittering effect. The quilt contains more than 100 different calicos and has a note attached in Almira's writing, "Quilt made by Talula

Gilbert Bottoms in late 1800's." Five other Glittering Star quilts
Talula made later have been found, all except one of which utilize
multiple calicoes in each star. That one is less interestingly pieced
with only one calico and the muslin in each star. Ironically, it is the
only one of these that is a "planned" quilt (made up in coordinated
colors) and beautifully framed on four sides with a pieced border.
These quilts emphasize both Talula's artistry and her frugality, for
the tiniest pieces of left-over material were used to create these
sophisticated "scrap" quilts.

Instead of the Star and Chain that Talula's youngest son was to
get, Gilbert and his wife Mayme, married in 1933 in Michigan, were
given two very special quilts thought to have been made between
1900 and 1912, after Talula, Tom and their seven children moved to
Sand Mountain, Alabama. One of these was the Dutch Rose, the
blocks made of solid deep green and red on a muslin background,
with the wide green, red, green sash emphasized at block points by
small nine-patch squares. It is so lovely one must wonder at Talula's
taking it with her to Battle Creek Sanitarium in Michigan, where
she went in 1912 for treatment of "female problems" so serious she
was not expected to live. While she was there another patient so admired the quilt he wanted to buy it, and Grandma, always generous, was willing to sell, but when the time came for her to leave, the
man could not be found, and the quilt came home with Talula.

The other special old quilt that went to Gilbert and Mayme was
the Honey Bee with its deep red and blue-green pieced and appliqued design set in a soft white muslin background. The patterned
squares are put together diagonally with alternating plain muslin
squares. Filled with thick cotton batting, the quilt is much heavier
and thicker than Talula's other quilts, so that one is amazed at the
small, even stitches in the 1/2 to 3/4-inch grid of the plain squares.
The superb quilting was done by eye measurement, judging from a
slight unevenness in grid width and absence of marking. It was
probably made about the same time as the Dutch Rose, 1900 to
1912, and could perhaps be accurately dated by the unusual solid
green, and the red which is deeper than Turkey red and tends to
bleed, though not to fade.

The scope of this paper does not permit discussion deserved by so
many more of Talula's quilts, nor of the family, economic, and
health problems brought on by World War I, the loss of two adult
sons, and the onset of the Great Depression when two other sons

lost their farms and there was danger of the old parents losing theirs. Even when Talula began having "curious spells" in the 1930s diagnosed as angina, she could rise above it for she never stopped piecing her quilts. Three <u>Lone Star</u> quilts pieced and quilted by Talula in late 1920s or early 1930s have been found, the material furnished to her by those for whom she was making them.

In 1934 Talula persuaded Burlie to drive her back to Georgia, to see once more the places and people she loved. Two brothers and one sister, cousins, and friends were still living there, and Talula came home ecstatic. She wrote a letter, alive with detail and excitement "To all my children and grandchildren in the US," perhaps to send round-robin, for the letter came back home to be put away in Tommie's childhood tool chest where she kept things she treasured. A significant part of that 18-page letter follows:

October 22, 1934 ...

At Johnnie May's we saw the old, old "Dahlia" quilt of my step grandmother's ...

'Then we went to my brother Bud's across the street and I spent that night with him, for I had not seen him. He was the one that came so near dying in the summer ...

"Well, while at Bud's I got to talking about the old quilt of my mother's that went to Bud. So Etta got it to show me, and I asked her to let me bring it home with me to try to get the pattern and make a square. So she did and I have made one square. It is very, very, pretty, and as none of us knew the name of it I have named it "The Life Boat," as the 5 blue corner pieces resemble oars more than anything. The center can be the boat and have 5 oars at each of the four corners. It is made in red, white, and blue."[16]

The <u>Lifeboat</u> (Figure 4) is an exceptional quilt, the 20-inch squares completely hand pieced and the calico oak-leaf crosses at the intersections of the 5½ muslin sash delicately appliqued. The five blue "oars" at each of the corners are pieced to four little tornado shaped funnels of white muslin, and the tiny red triangles to diamonds of muslin to form the "boats." A 5½-inch border of muslin all around makes the quilt's overall size 72 by 84 inches. The execution of the pattern is remarkable especially considering that Talula cut her own pattern pieces by the old quilt of her mother's. It is understandable she would want it quilted "nicely." For Talula that meant quilting it herself, although she had already begun taking quilts out to Mrs.

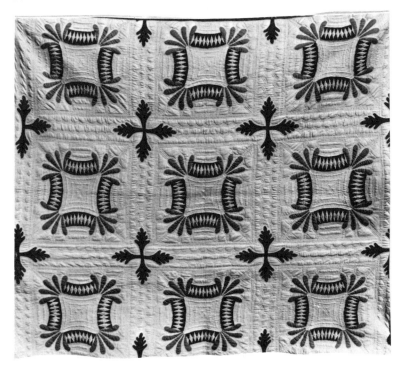

Fig. 4. The Lifeboat, c. 1935.

Brewer to have quilted for her.[17] She seems to have considered this one a special challenge, as it to prove to herself she could yet do the fine quilting she had done when younger, and it is indeed a masterpiece.

Letters from winter, spring, and summer 1935 show Talula, now 73, alive to every personal, family and community event, every joyous sight and sound of returning spring and bountiful summer, with only an occasional, unspecified reference to her quilting. Though there is talk of having to "put our place up for sale, for if we miss one payment the Land Bank will take it," Talula shows no alarm, and by October she has put the Lifeboat in her frame.

"I have to be very busy these days to get as much done on my quilt as I can before cold weather comes. I cannot go up to quilt when it is very cold; if I go up now will have to wrap up good. Have been wrapping the old overcoat around my

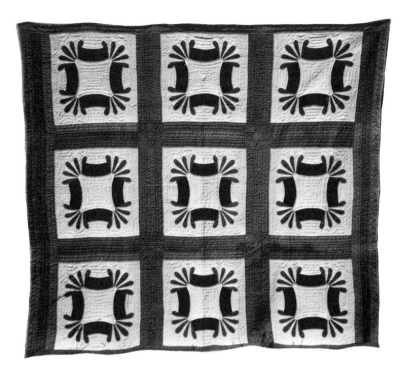

Fig. 5. Lifeboat II, c. 1936–1938.

feet and around my lap, tho will have more wrapping if I go
up tomorrow I think....[18]

Talula's quilting frame was set up in the big upstairs hall, 12 feet
wide, probably designed for her frame when the house plans were
drawn up by George, the brilliant son who died in a Georgia Army
camp in 1918. The hall was hot in summer, cold in winter, for the
only heat in the house was from the downstairs fireplaces and the
kitchen stove, but Gilbert remembers she almost always had a quilt
in her frame.

On October 12 in a letter to Mollie Ruth she wrote:
    "I have been working hard on my quilting while the
    weather is nice....

    I have my quilt about half out I think. If so I can get it out
    in three more weeks if I keep well and weather is so nice so I
    can stay upstairs. It is very pretty and I am trying to quilt it

nice, tho my fingers get so very sore and my wrist and hands get so tired. But by time I rest them until Monday will be ready to go it again as fast as I can. Have already used over 300 yards of thread, that is of the white thread, though not much of the red, as I do not quilt much in the red."[19]

From these letters it appears that Talula quilted the Lifeboat in about six weeks and used more than 600 yards of thread, the red only to outline the oak-leaf crosses. On the quilt's lining are the badges of her victory, several small bloodstains and one so large she has tried to rinse it out. Pinned to the quilt is a note in Almira's writing, "The Lifeboat, made about 1936 for Mollie Ruth by Mother Talula Bottoms, and quilted by her."

Another Lifeboat (Figure 5) soon followed this first one, not quite so intricately pieced or quilted, but perhaps more striking with its solid red boats, blue oars, and pieced peach and blue sash emphasized with 9-patch squares at intersection points. It was made for Almira and remains in her Alabama home, with her youngest son's family who inherited both the quilt and the home.

Talula's Lifeboat will be recognized as a variation of an old pattern today called Whig's Defeat, an 1850 example of which appears in Safford and Bishop's book.[20] An earlier example and one more comparable to Talula's and from nearer her locale, is described by Bets Ramsey in Uncoverings 1980.[21] She suggests in this article a relationship between the frugality of southern rural people, necessitated by harsh conditions after the Civil War, and a certain healing resourcefulness. Without doubt Talula's self-sufficiency was crucial in what appears to be the healing effect of her completion of the Lifeboat, and her chosen name for it is probably significant. Interviews and the exuberance reflected in many letters from this period, verify that from the mid-thirties until shortly before her death in 1946, her production was near incredible.

Talula would often have a dozen or more quilts in process, the pieces cut and kept in their individual Mars candy boxes which she had persuaded the proprietor of the traveling store, from whom she often bought material, to save for her. When a particular quilt she had made was so greatly admired, she would make two or three or six or eight more like it. Often she would let her granddaughters arrange the blocks on the big feather bed opposite the fireplace beside which she sat to piece her quilts. She kept many quilts and tops

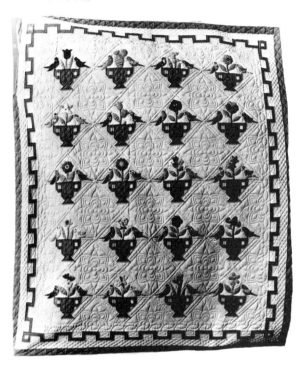

Fig. 6. The Garden Bouquet, pieced and appliqued 1940 by Talula Bottoms, quilted 1984 by Mary Slabaugh of Conewango Valley, New York.

folded away in a big round-top trunk to give to nieces or grand-children when they were married, to send to relatives when they were ill, or simply to give to friends, or neighbors, or anyone to reward them for some generous thing they had done. Three such quilts have been discovered in the Athens, Alabama area, where Talula and family moved in 1912, and it is possible many more could be found in Athens, Cullman County, and Fayette County areas, for more than one grandchild saw her simply give a quilt to some-one who "fell in love" with it. In the late 30s she donated three quilts to be raffled to buy land for a community building because many people in the area had no place to worship.[22]

Numerous letters from 1935 through 1945 show Talula not only working on several quilts at a time but making rugs, repotting porch and house plants every March, and growing yard and garden flowers so profuse and beautiful strangers would stop to admire and photograph them. A few letters indicate she was being asked to make quilts on order for people as far away as West Virginia and New York, who had seen quilts that had migrated there with her children. Interviews verify that she did indeed during this time complete her goal of appliquing little girl quilts for each of her 15 granddaughters, sometimes making them very special by sewing on "the buttons of Dad's baby dresses."[23]

One of the quilts Talula continued to make throughout the 1930s was the Garden Bouquet (Figure 6), a Nancy Page design by Florence LaGanke which ran as a weekly series in the *Nashville Banner* February–July 1932.[24] One of the first Garden Bouquets Talula made was for Mollie Ruth; it is now with her nephew's family in Alabama. Its delicate appliqued birds and flowers, its fine quilting outlining the patterned squares with the alternating plain squares quilted in a grid, and its unusual pieced urns and Greek key border, so pleased Talula and everyone who saw it that she set about to make one for each of her eight living children. She was still making these quilts in 1939 and possibly into the 40s, verified by a little rectangular template she had cut for the border from a postcard received from her older daughter.[25] Six Garden Bouquets have been found, four quilted by Talula and her two unquilted tops.

Talula had clipped and saved the complete series of patterns and instructions, twenty different flowers, two birds, the urns and the Greek key border. The brittle yellowed sheets were found after Almira's death in 1980. To each flower pattern Talula had pinned the little tissue paper templates she had cut for her own use; these are heavily perforated with pin holes, showing she had used them many times. Gilbert and Mayme inherited one of the later ones she made, an unquilted top. On it the hand stitching of the urn triangle half of the squares is of uneven quality and the Greek key border is unevenly pieced by sewing machine, attesting to the effects of aging on Talula's hands and eyes. That she would resolve to make eight of these quilts, with the delicate "laid work" so perfectly executed, is just one example of this little woman's great talent and generous heart.

One of the last quilts Talula mentions in her letters is Around the World. She completed the top in two weeks and "Papa likes it so much he wants to have it quilted and he keep it."[26] Other letters tell about her "curious spells" (one so severe she seemed gone for sure) but often end with, "but I can still do my quilt work," or "I may

Fig. 7. Thomas Jefferson and Talula Gilbert Bottoms, 1940, at their Athens, Alabama home. Photo courtesy George Bottoms.

make a good many quilts yet if I can keep my strength." A 1943 entry in her memoir says wistfully, "I sometimes wish I had them (her quilts) all here once more so I could see them."[27]

Almost everyone interviewed remembers Talula sitting beside the fireplace piecing quilts in her little home-made straight-back chair cushioned with two or three pillows, her quilting closet nearby filled with bags and boxes of scraps, and new cloth, sometimes whole bolts, bought for her, mail ordered or bought "off the truck,"as well as the boxes of cut pieces neatly arranged to lift off their little stacks. On warm days she would sit in her small rocking chair on the front porch, beside Tommie in his big one. She would have a Three Musketeers box on her lap, lifting off the little pieces with unbelievable speed and placing the finished squares in a basket beside her chair. While Tommie rocked and reminisced, or reflected on religion or the state of mankind, she would rock and sew, nodding in agreement and occasionally saying "Yes Tommie, you are absolutely right Tommie."[28] When company came, as it frequently did, she would get up and greet them warmly, make sure they were comfortable or fed, then sit again and sew while visiting. (Figure 7)

"She did not walk, she trotted about her work."[29] "She knew how to work without a wasted motion or a wasted moment,"[30] skills she had no doubt had to learn as a child and young woman, if she were to have any time left to piece quilts. She moved about her work with quick little steps, humming old hymns, waiting on "Papa" and her grandchildren, all of whom she called Honey Dear.[31] No one ever heard her raise her voice or complain. One granddaughter said, "I envisioned her as an earthly angel, she was so fragile, her voice soft, her face sweet and always smiling, even when she was in pain."[32]

Reading all her letters chronologically, one is impressed with the life-giving quality of her joyous craft. On June 21, 1941, she wrote:

> I started to be a little girl again yesterday ... I was out of the kind of cloth I was using in the quilt I was working on. So I got out patterns of one I made when a little girl and started on it as I had scraps ... It is now 5:30 and we are through in the kitchen, tho others are not up yet."[33]

She must have felt very rich indeed in these later years, for her sharp mind and her hands twisted with arthritis continued to create, often in complex and difficult patterns, to the end of her life.[34] She was thus able to be generous with this wealth of her own hands until her peaceful death at age 84.

Notes and References:

1. Talula Gilbert Bottoms' Memoir written in 1943, p. 4. This memoir, *Autobiography of Talula Gilbert Bottoms*, was privately published with an introduction and notes by Nancilu B. Burdick, granddaughter (Orchard Park, New York, The Apple Press, 1983). Library of Congress No. TX 1-350-638. A copy of this handwritten memoir has been placed in the Margaret Mitchell Library, Fayetteville, GA.
2. Bottoms, pp. 105–106.
3. Bottoms, pp. 12–13.
4. Bottoms, pp. 42–43.
5. Bottoms, pp. 8–9.
6. Bottoms, p. 10.
7. Bottoms, pp. 14, 43.

8. Bottoms, p. 88.

9. Bottoms, p. 46. (Talula's Orange Bud proves elusive, although one like it made in Georgia in 1864 has been found in Fayetteville, GA. The granddaughter who inherited Talula's quilt died in 1979 and her seven children are widely scattered.)

10. Carleton L. Safford and Robert Bishop, *America's Quilts and Coverlets* (New York, E.P. Dutton, 1980) p. 161.

11. Talula gave this remarkable quilt to her granddaughter who fell in love with the Rocky Mountain in the 1930s, since the Rocky Mountain had already been promised to Almira, this quilt, date unknown, was its substitute, and is just as striking.

12. Letter Talula Bottoms to Mollie Ruth Bottoms, Dec. 11, 1940.

13. This quilt may have been bound with a sewing machine turned by hand. On pages 20 and 21 of her memoir Talula describes such a machine and says, "I used ... that machine of theirs after we were married." The Feather and the Rocky Mountain appear to have been bound about the same time, possibly several years later than they were quilted (1892 and 1893). Among Talula's letters was found a receipt and guarantee for a Standard Sewing Machine (Cleveland, OH) "Sold to T.J. Bottoms on Nov. 9, 1895."

14. Mrs. A.P. Travers, "Grandmother's Quilts," *Southern Agriculturist*, June 1, 1928, p. 1 (loaned by Ruth B. Potts, Florence, AL).

15. Letter, Talula Bottoms to Mollie Ruth Bottoms, Oct. 9, 1940.

16. Letter, Talula Bottoms to Mollie Ruth Bottoms, Oct. 22, 1934.

17. Letter, Talula Bottoms to Mollie Ruth Bottoms, Feb. 3, 1935. (Mrs. A.I. Brewer of the Athens area did shell quilting for $1.50 each, $5.00 "by the piece," but she did not do the fine quilting Talula wanted.)

18. Letter, Talula Bottoms to Mollie Ruth Bottoms, Oct. 6, 1935.

19. Letter, Talula Bottoms to Mollie Ruth Bottoms, Oct. 12, 1935.

20. Safford and Bishop, p. 121.

21. Bets Ramsey, "Design Invention in Country Quilts of Tennessee and Georgia," *Uncoverings 1980*, (Mill Valley, CA, American Quilt Study Group, 1981) pp. 49–50.

22. Mrs. Gladie Coffman, telephone interview, Athens, AL, July 2, 1984. (Mrs. Coffman has a Bear Paw Talula gave her for helping with the raffle.)

23. Letter, Estelle Fernandez to Nancilu Burdick, June, 1984. The little girl quilts are Colonial Girl, Dutch Doll, and Sunbonnet Sue.

24. Florence LaGanke, "Nancy Page Quilt Club," the *Nashville Banner*, Feb.–July, 1932 (loaned by Ruth B. Potts).

25. Almira's postcard from which the heavily perforated template was cut, reports the death of her nephew's child "this morning." The child died in April, 1939. (Template found among Garden Bouquet clippings and patterns loaned by Ruth B. Potts.)
26. Letters, Talula Bottoms to Mollie Ruth Bottoms, May 17, 1941, and May 27, 1941.
27. Bottoms, p. 49.
28. Letter, Anna Swart to Nancilu Burdick, July, 1984; also telephone interview, Mary Wentworth. Anna and Mary lived in close proximity to their grandparents in the early 30s and from 1940 until Talula and Tommie died, 1946 and 1947.
29. Interview, Charles Bottoms, Little Genessee, NY, Sept., 1983.
30. Interview, Gilbert A. Bottoms, Sedro Wooley, WA, Nov., 1983.
31. Interview, Margaret Avery, Boulder City, NV, July, 1984.
32. Letter, Anna Swart to Nancilu Burdick, July, 1984.
33. Letter, Talula Bottoms to Mollie Ruth Bottoms, June, 1941.
34. Talula's granddaughter, Martha Hammack of Punta Gorda Isles, FL, inherited several of Talula's unfinished quilt tops and several boxes of her cut pieces, from her mother who had received them from Talula before her death. One star quilt, Talula had begun and Martha has just completed, has a large flower pieced to each star, its gathered petals filling up the center so that the star points look like arrowheads. The same pattern is called Dahlia in Dorothy Fager's *The Book of Sampler Quilts* (Radnor, PA, Childton Book Co.), 1983, p. 94.

    Among other quilts, the pieces cut, or tops unfinished, are Double Wedding Ring, Pilot's Wheel, Glittering Star and Improved Nine Patch. The last year or two of her life she made at least 15 quilt tops in "easier" patterns, hand pieced with larger pieces and longer stitches. Eight Grecian Star and seven Sunflower quilts made during this period have been found, both patterns of which require sewing of unusual shapes and curved pieces!

Dyes in American Quilts Made Prior to 1930, with Special Emphasis on Cotton and Linen

James N. Liles

Even though cotton and linen (the cellulose fibers) were more difficult, time consuming, and expensive to dye than wool and silk (protein fibers), every conceivable color, hue, and shade was possible by the period 1750–1850. Indeed, many of the best dyes were available before 1630. The vast majority of 18th and 19th century dye manuals contained as many or more recipes for cotton and linen as for wool.[1,2,3] This undoubtedly reflects the increasing importance of cotton in Europe, and therefore America, after the 1600s.

Many of the early cotton and linen dyes were fairly fast to both washing and light while others were not so good. Much of one book, of several written in the 19th century, is devoted to the cleaning and redying of faded articles of clothing.[4]

Indian cotton calicoes, when first introduced into Europe in the early 1600s were quite justifiably considered one of the marvels of the world. By the late 1600s, imported printed cotton cloth for clothing became very fashionable in all of Europe. Wash and lightfast colors on these printed Indian fabrics included red, gray, black, purple-brown, brown, and blue. The yellows and greens were relatively fugitive to light owing to the use of turmeric for the yellow(s).[5] Cotton was the major fabric fiber in India from very early times. How early cotton dyeing occurred in India is not known, but fragments of mordanted yarn (for dyeing) were unearthed at Mohenjo Daro in the Indus Valley of India, dated roughly 2,000 BC.[6,7] Indian supremacy in cotton dyeing probably resulted from (1) early settlement, (2) a large population and labor force, (3) the presence of wild cotton and the best dye bearing plants, (4) a very intelligent people, (5) the presence of the necessary natural

James M. Liles: 2142 Cherokee Blvd, Knoxville, TN 37919

mordants, (6) an unusual love of color, and (7) a philosophy of life which said if it takes a year to dye it right then let it take a year.

The later perfection of the completely washfast and lightfast Turkey Red process by Persian and Greek dyers in the Levant by about 1600 resulted in importation of large quantities of this material in Europe, especially thread for sewing and embroidery. This trade continued until well into the 1750s by which time the French finally unravelled all of the secrets of this very complicated Oriental process. In addition to the use of Turkey red, European dyeing and printing of cotton advanced at a remarkable rate from 1700 on, as the development of chemistry was at a more advanced state there.

Available evidence indicates that quilting materials used early on in America were mostly imported from Europe (England, primarily), and therefore of European, Indian, or Asian origin. A note to this effect from Brunswick Town, North Carolina (occupied 1726–1776) indicates that the cloth used for making clothing was virtually all imported from England. Bales of cloth from England were protected from possible theft by lead baleing seals impressed with the name of the city and the manufacturer. Archeological digs have unearthed a number of these lead seals, one with the impression "Lynch & Co., London."[8]

Virtually all of the professional dyers in America before 1840 or so were either trained in Europe or employed by those who had such training. These dyers preferred to continue using the dyes they were trained with in Europe.[9] Also, most of the available dye manuals in the 17th, 18th, and 19th centuries were written by Europeans, and if by an American, most of the recipes were copied from the European dye manuals. In addition, Europeans attempted to retain sales of their goods to us by imposing what was fashionable, thus inhibiting development and use of our own natural dyeplants.[10] Because other crops were more profitable in America, dye plants were not culti-vated commercially during the 17th, 18th and 19th centuries except for indigo in South Carolina.[11]

The extent of home dyeing of cotton and linen in America prior to 1850 with native or imported dyes is not well documented. Native dyeplants would have provided golds and yellow-browns, off greens and green-grays, grays and browns. Most of the yellows other than black oak bark would have been rather fugitive to light.

That manufactured cloth, imported or domestic, was available at relatively early dates, even in the backwoods, is better documented. The Knoxville, Tennessee *Gazette* in 1796 advertised bolts of commercial cloth.[12] And in 1840 the Merrimac and Hamilton Mills in Lowell, Mass. produced more than 250,000 yards of cotton printed in madder colors.[13] Indeed, James Franklin (brother of Benjamin Franklin) is reported to have dyed and printed calico in America in the 1720s, and indigo-blue resists were produced during the 18th century.[14,15]

My interpretation of the preceeding is that most of the dyed quilting materials up until at least 1800 came from commercially produced cloth, and all of the printed cloth from settlement to 1930 was commercial.

In 1856 William Henry Perkin, an English chemist, produced quite by accident the first synthetic dye, mauvine, from Aniline, a coal tar product. This important discovery marked the beginning of the end for most natural and mineral dyes. Indeed, discovery of new synthetics was so rapid that except for isolated areas such as the Southern mountains, and during World War I when German synthetic dyestuffs were cut off, only about fifteen natural and mineral dyes were still commercially profitable by the turn of the 20th century. The early synthetic dyes, though possessing rather poor lightfastness, produced more standard, predictable colors than natural dyes, and were cheaper and easier to apply. On the other hand, one general characteristic of the older natural dyes was that they usually faded true—becoming lighter and often more mellow with time. This was not true of the early synthetics and some of our modern synthetics. Many early synthetics turned rather hideous colors when faded, not resembling the original color at all. Several thousand different coal-tar dyestuffs had been produced by 1925, with perhaps 100 or so fast to light and washing.[16] Many of the poorer dyes were used only for a few years, never to be produced again. Far more of these dyes were used for wool and silk than for cotton and linen.[17]

In America the first packaged dyes were put on the market by Howe and Stevens in 1863. These were various natural dyestuffs ground to a fine powder and mixed with a ground mordant. By 1864, however, five of their "family dye colors" were imported European synthetics, including magenta and mauve. Again, these were less adequate in cotton than wool, but by about 1880 packaged synthetic Diamond dyes could be bought at every drugstore and country store in the most remote parts of the United States, and some of these were reasonably good cotton dyes.[18] Of course, collecting plants such as goldenrod, black oak bark, and sumac was much cheaper!

The dyes

Red: The very best, fastest, and most sought after red from 1600 to 1930 was Turkey Red, and the simpler madder reds were inferior only in brilliance and complexity of color. Several plants of the family Rubiaceae (madder, chay, morinda) contain the principle dyeing ingredient which is known as alizarin. Indian dyers probably produced fast madder reds by 2000 B.C., and they may have developed the Turkey Red process also, though this is usually credited to the Persian, Turkish, and Greek dyers along the area of the Mediterranean known as the Levant in about 1600. The process was much more complicated than simple madder red. It originally involved some 13–20 tricky steps over a three to four month period. Ingredients used in various of the steps (from 1600–1880) included madder, cattle, sheep, or camel's dung, rancid olive oil, castor oil, sesame seed oil, or lard, soda ash, tannin, alum, chalk, and often blood. The brightening process which produced the brilliant, fiery shades included boiling for several hours under pressure with soap solutions, and often tin salts. Even the best dye houses had reasonably frequent failures. Turkey Red was expensive, but it would last until the cloth was in tatters, and it did not fade or bleed out on surrounding white areas.

So complicated was the process that it took literally every country in Europe 150 years to steal away and master this Oriental process. The French were first, in 1750. The color has been variously described as a soft blue red with inner glowing fire and as shades from sombre to luminescent. By 1900 the process had been shortened to about seven days, but with quite elaborate equipment and slight sacrifice in fastness. It is the most complex of any dye known, ancient or modern, and its entire chemistry has never been totally elucidated, mostly because it was entirely replaced by the fast vat and developed reds by 1940, at which point further study of its chemistry ceased. It went under the names Turkey Red, Levant, Rouge turc, rouge des Indes, Adrianopolis, and Adrianople Red. Adrianople, an ancient Turkish city, was a major center for its production.

Because of the time and expense in producing Turkey Red, some other very pretty fancy reds were also used, though rather fugitive to light. I cannot help but think that some of them showed up in quilts, and they were probably relatively satisfactory for quite a few years if in the bedroom of a dimly lighted cabin. The safflower colors faded true, but the red woods fade to a reddish brown. The redwoods include Brazilwood (peachwood, Nicaragua, sappanwood, Pernambuco, Fernambouc, Bois de Bresil), and Barwood (Camwood, Sanderswood, sandalwood). The best way the redwoods were used was to combine them with common madder red, and this produced a good and lasting red. The excellent cochineal, kermes, and lac reds (insect dyes), were much used on wool and silk, but rarely on cotton and linen. Fugitive reds included annotto, pokeberries, and bloodroot. Annotto (reddish-orange) fades rather true.

Some old quilts may show considerably more brown colors than they contained originally. Not only do the redwoods fade to a reddish brown, but so do some of the early synthetic dyes produced from 1860–1900, such as neutral red and Congo Red. Another early aniline red, magenta, fades to a rather ugly purple-brown. Congo red was discovered by Boettger in 1884, and it was a very easy to use, cheap, direct dye. It dyed level and a faded article could be easily redyed. Because of this, many Indians (India) turned to it and away from British produced Turkey Red, depressing the industry, particularly in Manchester, and putting thousands of people out of work.[19,20]

From 1870–1930, several somewhat fugitive commercial and home dyes were pawned off as Turkey Red. For example, Ramsey reported the story of a Georgia lady buying Turkey Red powder at the store in Calhoun. The time was between 1873–1907.[21] The "Turkey Red" powder was probably Congo Red.

Between 1910–20 the brilliant and fast anthraquinone vat dyes were developed, including red, and these were available in America after World War I. Also, a very good developed red, Paranitraniline red, a naphthol dye, was in commercial production by 1918, and much used in place of Turkey Red by 1920.[22] It produced an excellent bright shade of red, somewhat more yellow and less blue in tone than Turkey Red. Occasionally methods were used to make it bluer in tone. The color was extremely fast to washing, and it did not bleed into interwoven white when scoured in hot soap solutions. Vat reds at this time were also fast and brilliant, though they did not possess the complex beauty of Turkey Red. Thus, fast non-fading brilliant reds from 1918 or so on included Turkey Red, developed red, and vat red.

By 1928 at least 100 synthetic red dyes had been produced, but only about four or five passed all tests of fastness.[23]

Blue: Properly executed, the number one blue dye during the period of this paper as well as for probably the last 5000 years is indigo. The earliest dated specimen may be a fragment of dyed linen from Thebes, dated about 3500 BC.[24] Indigo is still used for the finest Japanese kimonos, African textiles, fading blue jeans, and by modern fiber artists. Indigo may be used to dye full pieces, and it can also be printed.[25,26,27] Indigo may be dyed on cotton and linen from the palest blue to almost a purple black, and it is quite fast to washing and light except in the palest shades. Indigo is, and always has been an expensive dye, and it takes some experience to use well. At one point in the 18th century indigo cost $2.25 per pound, while logwood cost only six cents per pound.[28] Therefore, the temptation for the home dyer to use logwood blue in cotton and linen must have been great. Logwood blues are pretty, newly made, but they are fugitive, fading to a light pink-purple. After 1820–30, Prussian blue, a mineral dye, became available in America. It was produced first by Mauvier in France in 1753, and rediscovered in Germany about 1800. Like all mineral dyes, it was used in fabric printing. Prussian blue was also called Napolean's blue, and Berlin Blue, and its various shades had names, such as sky blue and royal blue. It is quite lightfast and relatively wash fast unless treated with very alkaline laundry soaps. If destroyed by repeated washing the remaining color is iron buff (reddish brown). None of the early synthetic blues for cotton and linen were very good until about 1920. Rather satisfactory synthetics of this period included methylene blue, toluidine blue, New Diamond Indigo Blue, and Indanthrene blue (a vat dye).

Yellow: Clear, clean yellows on cotton and linen were a problem up to about 1840 with none showing excellent lightfastness. The best of this period included weld and old fustic, and by about 1800 American black oak bark. Weld and black oak bark were the most lightfast of the old vegetable yellows. Other home dyed yellows of the period could include peach leaves, white aster, goldenrod, coreoposis, smartweed, whiteash, barberry, osage orange, marigolds, Queen Anne's lace, broom sedge, Persian berries (used in calico printing) and many others. If the dyer were willing to accept a golden tan, or yellow tan, the color would be more lasting. The same dyestuffs were used, but more tannin (brownish) was used in the mordanting. Indian calico yellow, as well as greens (yellow overdyed with indigo) usually contained turmeric for the yellow. Turmeric dyes directly, i.e., without a mordant, and is a very clear yellow. However, it is a fugitive to light, and calico leaf prints, originally green, would become blue eventually as the turmeric faded out. In fact, many old tapestries, coverlets, quilts, etc., show more red, blue, and brown than they originally contained, and less yellow, green, orange, and gray.

Potassium dichromate (chrome) produced in 1797 made possible the production of the clear, clean, brilliant mineral dye known as chrome yellow. It was produced commercially in America by about 1840. Chrome yellow is quite fast, but it is also poisonous, and was so particularly to factory workers producing large yardages of the material. The dye was used in commercial production until about 1910.[29] It was also used to color paper, and our "Greenback dollars" were dyed with chrome green (Prussian blue overdyed with chrome yellow) from about 1850–1900.[30] It can be discharged, as is the case with all mineral dyes, and so could be used in calico printing. Unless exposed to heavy concentrations of coal smoke, chrome yellow remained bright, but because of its poisonous nature would have been replaced by early synthetic yellows if they had been any good. Napier's book (1875) listed no recipes using synthetic yellow dyes for cotton and linen.[31] Fast vat synthetic yellows became available shortly after the end of World War I as did fast sulfur yellows.

Brown: When it comes to brown, tan, fawns, and olives, the traditional cotton dyes were nearly as fast as the best of our modern dyes. Indian cutch, in my opinion, surpasses the modern dyes in beauty. This dye is obtained from the Indian acacia tree (*Acacia catechu*). It is sometimes referred to as catechu or Bombay or Bengal catechu. A similar substance is obtained from gambier (*Uncaria gambir*).[7] Cutch was used in Indian calico for centuries and was in use in European printed cottons by about 1800. Cutch was still used in commercial American dyeing until about 1930. Other very good natural brown dyes on properly tannin-alum mordanted cotton and linen included black walnut or butternut hulls, and alder or red maple bark, and many home dyers produced a reasonably good brown with tea. Fast natural brown was also obtained by dyeing iron mordanted material with madder (this can also produce gray).

By 1850 or so manganese bronze (bistre), a mineral dye, became available and was used until 1910 or slightly later. Shades from light bronze to full seal brown could be produced, and they were fast. This material was also used as a gunstock stain. Mineral khaki became available at about the same time. It is a mixture of chromium and iron oxides. Synthetic sulfur khaki appeared in about 1912, just in time to replace mineral khaki of our army uniforms. (All mineral dyes roughen the fabric, at least slightly.)[33]

Bismark brown, a synthetic aniline dye produced in the late 1860s, while quite beautiful newly made, was not lightfast. Good synthetic sulfur and vat browns were available by 1930, but the easier to use direct browns were not so good, particularly to washing fastness, though by this time they were fast to light.

Gray, black and steel: The gray and black dyes from antiquity until nearly the beginning of the 20th century were iron tannates, i.e., fibers treated with iron salts and vegetable tannins as from sumac, hemlock, or galls. Properly done, these grays and blacks often lasted for years, though they could revert to a rusty color if subjected to excessive exposure and sunlight. By 1600 logwood from Central and South America was often added along with iron tannate producing a blacker and sometimes more permanent color. Properly mordanted with chrome, logwood was used to dye inexpensive blacks on wool up to about 1940.[35]

Iron mordants do cause premature deterioration of natural fibers somewhat, and this is even more true of silk than cotton. Sometimes an old quilt will show disintegration of gray or black material while the remainder of the fabric is sound. Mordanting or weighting with tin salts also produces this effect.

Good natural blacks were also produced by dyeing black walnut over deep indigo. This produced a nice dark permanent purple-black. Also, the three primary colors were often combined to produce black, i.e., madder, fustic, and indigo. Synthetic aniline (coal tar) black dates back to 1863.[36] It is formed by oxidation of aniline on the fiber being dyed, and was a very fast black on cotton, and used especially for calico printing. If the oxidation of the aniline was not complete, the fiber eventually turned green, but this was a problem only with the earliest product. Thus, many good, fast blacks and grays were available before 1930.

Compound Colors: Prior to the advent of synthetic dyes, most greens, oranges, and purples were produced by overdyeing one color with another. Thus, most greens were produced by overdyeing indigo with a good yellow dye or vice versa. Few of these cotton greens were satisfactory for long exposure to light; old fustic, weld, and black oak bark generally were the best, though turmeric was also often used. Mairet considered vegetable cotton greens unsatisfactory for the home dyer.[37] A very fast mineral dye or mineral-natural combination appeared about 1840 and lasted until probably the 1920s since it withstood exposure so well (it was also used for outdoor green awning material well into the 20th century). This green dye was either prussian blue or indigo overdyed with chrome yellow. Obviously, these greens would hold up very well in quilting materials. Greens were also produced by overdyeing fustic with Prussian blue, but these would not be as lightfast as the chrome greens. Synthetic aniline greens were listed in dye manuals by 1875, but the early products were not particularly fast to light or washing. However, by 1920 several good developed and vat greens were on the market.

Orange: A rather beautiful natural orange on cotton was gotten with annotto, obtained from a South American plant, but it is very fugitive to light. It did fade true, but very rapidly. This same dye was also used to color butter and cheese, and our early terrible looking white oleomargarine during World War II. Even so, I imagine annotto was occasionally used in early quilting materials because natural oranges are sadly lacking. Compound oranges produced on cotton and linen with madder and a yellow dye would eventually fade mostly to the red. This was not the case with wool dyed the same way. The most permanent oranges, prior to good synthetics were antimony orange and chrome orange which became available between 1820 and 1840. This was produced by heating chrome yellow in an alkaline solution. As is true of most of the other colors, really good synthetic oranges did not appear until about 1920.

Purple: Beautiful natural purples on wool were gotten by dyeing with cochineal red and then overdyeing with indigo. Cotton, however, does not take cochineal well and madder red-indigo purples, while fast, were not so outstandingly pretty. Another early and fast Indian purple (later called Egyptian purple) was produced by mordanting with both iron and alum and then dyeing with madder. The color is sort of a purple-brown. Cotton dyed in very deep shades with indigo alone produced a very striking violet purple, and getting this effect depended partly on the skill of the dyer. Prussian blue (sky blue shade) overdyed with safflower pink produced a beautiful lilac and, in spite of the fugitive nature of safflower, this dye is listed in dye manuals as late as 1885.[38] In compound form the safflower fades more slowly than when present alone. Tin mordanted logwood cotton purples were also used from the 1600s to the 1880s. These were also quite pretty, but fugitive both to washing and light, fading to a light pink. I feel quite certain, though, that I have seen faded logwood purples on both old quilts and coverlets. Again, fast synthetic purples were not available in America until after World War I.

Finally, in discussing compound colors, it should be pointed out that sometimes a natural dye was combined with a synthetic, or two or more synthetics were combined![39] Any and all methods were employed to get just that correct shade or improvement in fastness. Many of our modern dye colors could be much more beautiful if this soft of effort and expense were more frequently expended.

The dyes discussed in this paper cover the period from the colonization of America to 1930. In conclusion I might add that I have spent the past five years researching and reproducing these traditional cotton and linen dyes, as well as a few of the early synthetics.

Work on Turkey Red alone has been in progress the entire time, and only now do I feel that my product is satisfactory in all respects. I do not regret a single moment spent in this work. Seeing the colors, newly made, has impressed me with the fact that the traditional dyes were "good enough." Indeed many of them far surpass our modern dyes in sheer, subtle beauty, if not in fastness. But then who knows what our modern quilts will look like 100 years hence? No dye is completely fade resistant. As to beauty, the natural dyes are not pure colors, thus they rarely clash when placed side by side. Proper mixing of modern dyes could effect the same result, but this is all too seldom done. The fact that human beings would spend three or four months to produce a suitable dye simply illustrates that food, shelter, and clothing are not enough—color is also necessary!

Notes and References:

1. Edward Bancroft, *Experimental Researches Concerning the Philosophy of Permanent Colours*, London: 1794, throughout.
2. E. Bermis, *The Dyer's Companion*, New York: Dover Publishers, Inc., 1973. Unabridged republication of the 2nd. (1815) ed., published by E. Duyckinck, New York. Introduction by Rita Adrosko. Throughout.
3. James N. Napier, *A Manual of Dyeing and Dyeing Receipts*, London: Charles Griffin and Co., 1875, pp. 356–407.
4. William Tucker, *The Family Dyer and Scourer*, London: Paternoster Row, 1822, throughout.
5. Mattiebelle Gittinger, *Master Dyers to the World*, Washington, D.C., The Textile Museum, 1982, p. 22.
6. Gittinger, p. 19.
7. Franco Brunello, *The Art of Dyeing in the History of Mankind*, Cleveland: Phoenix Dye Works, 1973, p. 67.
8. *Newsletter, Brunswick County Historical Society*, Box 632, Shallotte, N.C., Vol. III (I); February, 1963, p. 2.
9. Adrosko, p. 6.
10. Adrosko, p. 6.
11. Adrosko, p. 15.

12. William F. Rogers, *Life on the Kentucky—Tennessee Frontier Near the End of the Eighteenth Century*, 1925, University of Tennessee Masters Thesis, p. 32 and 60.
13. Adrosko, p. 23.
14. Stuart Robinson, A History of Dyed Textiles, Cambridge: The MIT Press, 1969, p. 32.
15. Dena Katzenberg, *Blue Traditions*, (Indigo Dyed Textiles and Related Cobalt Glazed Ceramics from the 17th through the 19th Century), Baltimore: The Baltimore Museum of Art, 1973, throughout.
16. Charles E. Pellew, *Dyes and Dyeing*, New York: Robert M. McBride & Co., 1928, p. 59.
17. Pellew, throughout.
18. Sidney M. Edelstein, *Historical Notes on the Wet-Processing Industry*, Dexter Chemical Corporation, 1972, p. 90.
19. J.M. Matthews, *Application of Dyestuffs to Textiles, Paper, Leather and Other Materials*, New York: John Wiley & Sons, Inc., p. 275.
20. Pellew, p. 74.
21. Bets Ramsey, "Cotton Country: Redbud Georgia 1873–1907," In *Quilt Close-Up—Five Southern Views*, Chattanooga: The Hunter Museum of Art, 1983, p. 20.
22. Matthews, p. 322.
23. Pellew, pp. 58–59.
24. Matthews, p. 8.
25. Gittinger, throughout.
26. Katzenberg, pp. 25–35.
27. Florence H. Pettit, *America's Indigo Blues*, New York: Hastings House Publishers, 1974, pp. 17–24.
28. Adrosko, p. 8.
29. Matthews, p. 513.
30. Charles E. Pellew, *Dyeing for Craftsmen, II. The Dyestuffs of our Ancestors*, Handicraft 5(6), 1912, p. 94.
31. Napier, pp. 364–366.
32. Adrosko, p. 40.
33. Matthews, p. 513.
34. Pellew, p. 75–76.
35. Adrosko, p. 47.
36. Matthews, p. 451.
37. Ethel M. Mairet, *Vegetable Dyes*, New York: Chemical Publishers Co., Inc., 1939, p. 46.
38. J.J. Hummel, *The Dyeing of Textile Fabrics*, London: Cassell & Co., Ltd., 1885, p. 356.
39. Matthews, p. 263.

A Century of Fundraising Quilts: 1860-1960

Dorothy Cozart

Until recently, comparatively little had been written about women's quiltmaking activities which made money either for themselves or for charitable causes. Fundraisers, which I am defining as those quilts made specifically for the purpose of soliciting money from individuals or groups, were virtually ignored in quilt histories written before 1970. *Quilts in America*,[1] published in 1974, pictures two quilts that probably were fundraisers, and identifies one as such in the caption beneath the photo. *America's Quilts and Coverlets*[2] also pictures two fundraisers and identifies them as such. *Three Hundred Years of Canada Quilts*[3] pictures and describes one fundraiser in some detail and also indicates that many more have been made in Canada. *A People and Their Quilts*[4] not only gives a typical description of the method used in making and raising money on a quilt, it also mentions several instances in which individuals and groups in Tennessee made and sold quilts, or did quilting, then gave the money to churches. Quilt catalogs have identified and pictured several fundraisers, and *Kentucky Quilts 1800-1900*,[5] *Quilts and Carousels*,[6] and *Nova Scotia Workbasket*[7] contain brief discussions of fundraising quilts. Nancy J. Rowley's paper in *Uncoverings 1982*[8] deals with fundraising quilts made for a specific purpose, "Red Cross Quilts for the Great War." My paper is an expansion of all these findings and will discuss what I have chosen to call "group fundraisers," those made by a group of people, rather than by individuals, as were some of the Red Cross quilts which both Nancy Rowley and I have located. All the quilts used for this paper have been identified as fundraisers either by oral or written documentation and, with two exceptions to be noted later, were made between 1860 and 1960.

Dorothy Cozart: Rt. 1, Box 93, Waukomis, OK 73773

The following is from "The History of Olive Hill Church," published in the *Holton* (Kansas) *Recorder* in July, 1927. This excerpt,
about the fundraising activity of a small Methodist church, is what
sparked my interest in fundraising quilts.

> From the files of the *Holton Recorder*, W. E. Beighter has se-
> cured these items. In the issue of July 23, 1883, "The good
> people of Olive Hill have raised $1600 in funds to build a
> church edifice."
>
> June 4, 1884, "Olive Hill will have an ice cream supper
> June 16. They will sell the wheel quilt at that time, the pro-
> ceeds will be used to finish the church."
>
> If memory serves us right, this same wheel quilt was a de-
> sign of a wheel in red on foundation of white for which
> names were solicited with 10 cents for placing the name on
> the tire, 25 cents on a spoke, and 50 cents on the hub.
> Much money was raised in this way, different ladies vieing
> with each other in securing the most names and money on
> their block. ... Mr. Stauffer was the auctioneer who dis-
> posed of the wheel quilt which sold for twenty-five dollars
> to John Dix.[9]

Unfortunately, the quilt itself has not been located, but this writing
is very representative of the written and oral accounts of the signature fundraisers that I have subsequently discovered. This account is
also typical in that the quilt was made as a fundraiser by a group of
church women. My research indicates that most fundraising quilts
were made to benefit churches, with the funds being used in various
ways, including the building of a new church.

Most of the signature quilts located were made using a circular or
wheel design that has a center in which names are written, with
more names radiating out from the "hub." Some of the wheels are
appliqued and the names appear between the spokes and/or outside
the tire. (#14, #16, #25) One circle is a pieced Sunburst; the names
are embroidered in the center and on each of the diamonds of the
"burst." (#4) Some of the circles are sunflowers and other flowers,
and some are Dresden Plate or Friendship Ring.

Designs that are not circular include the Single and Double Irish
Chain, the Glorified Nine-Patch, the Double T and Crown of
Thorns. Beehives and Seagulls, composed of blocks embroidered
with beehives and seagulls and names written in other blocks, is the

Fig. 1. A block of the fundraiser quilt made by the women of the First Methodist Church, Bartlesville, Oklahoma in 1915. Photo by Bryan Gammon.

newest quilt included in this paper, made in 1964. (#49) The oldest quilt was made about 1850 and is a red appliqued circle with white "petals" inside the circle. (#1)

Red was the most common color used in the signature quilts, usually red on white, although one is white on red.[10] (#13) Other colors used with white are orange, blue, old rose and gold. Only one quilt's description noted the significance of the colors, a 1911 quilt in Montgomery County, New York, which was settled by people from the Netherlands. It used orange, blue and white, the colors of Netherland's flag. (#20)

On no quilt yet discovered are the individual makers of the quilt identified as such. However, stories that accompany the quilts often do identify makers. Sometimes the names were embroidered by one person, and her name may be remembered. One quilt has the names of the women who quilted it quilted into the border, but this also is a remembered fact only. (#31) In some cases the woman who was responsible for the signatures on a certain block may have her name in the hub, but that information is not noted on the quilt. An indication of how hard these mostly "anonymous" women worked obtaining signatures is given in an account in the Linden, Iowa, Methodist Church *Centennial, 1882–1982.* This was sent to me by Mary Barton, whose grandmother, Allie Lisle, is mentioned.[11]

> Names cost 10¢ to be embroidered by the women and Allie
> Lisle twisted most of the arms in town. When Martha Gil-
> more had the quilt, she listed all the names and put in some
> not there until all blocks were filled.[12]

There are 169 names on that quilt. (#28)

The number of names on a quilt may indicate that it was a fund-raiser. Many quilts found have at least 150 names on them and a number have more than 400. Three quilts contain more than 1000 signatures, and, in two instances, names of churches and organiza-tions as well as individuals. (#6, #9) The quilt containing the most signatures is the one called "The Refrigerator Quilt."

The Refrigerator Quilt was made by the Trinity Evangelical Church in Kansas City in 1935 and 1936. The purpose was to collect money to buy a kerosene refrigerator for Juanita and Wilbur Harr, who were going as missionaries to Nigeria. All the churches in the Kansas Conference of the Evangelical Church were contacted, and, as a result, there are approximately 1860 signatures on the Sunflower quilt. Enough money was raised to buy the refrigerator, cover freight costs and buy some kerosene. The quilt was then given to the Harrs and they used it while in Africa and for many years after they re-turned. It now belongs to the daughter of Mrs. Arthur J. Brunner, the instigator and moving force behind this money-making project. (#43)

A number of fundraisers contain few or no signatures. For ex-ample, a Log Cabin made in 1866 in Missouri raised money to aid needy families of ex-Confederate soldiers. "Feed the Hungry" is written with sequins in the center of the quilt. (#3) The Kentucky Baptist Orphans Home quilt was constructed in blocks, although it was a Crazy Quilt, because churches, Sunday School classes, asso-ciations and individual members of Baptist churches were asked to contribute and put their names on a block. (#6) The Monroeville (Ohio) Town Hall Quilt, made in 1888, contains names and busi-nesses of Monroeville merchants and had a central painted velvet block picturing the town hall. (#8) Quilts made in Michigan (#39) and New York (#20) also have pictures of buildings as central blocks. Mary Conroy states in *Three Hundred Years of Canada Quilts* that she has seen several quilts which have a central panel of an embroidered church, school or other building.[13]

Two quilts, one made in Oklahoma and one in Kansas, contain few signatures and only the provenance of the quilts reveals that they were fundraisers. (#29, #41) Funds were raised in identically the same way for both, and both were made at about the same time by Methodist women's groups. Each woman pieced a block, choosing her own pattern, and she paid a penny for each pattern piece. The woman whose block contained the most pieces won the quilt. I am convinced that more of these quilts are still in existence, but no one remembers that they were fundraisers.

Funds were usually raised in two ways: first, individuals donated money so that their signatures would be on the quilt, and second, the finished quilt was sold or raffled. As was described in the account of the Olive Hill quilt above, the placement on the wheel sometimes determined the amount paid for a signature. The center was usually the highest, with 25¢ and 50¢ being a common amount paid for that space. Otherwise, 10¢ was the amount most often mentioned and 2¢ was the least amount I found. (#38) Usually from $25 to $100 was collected for the signatures. However, the 81 blocks for the Baptist Orphans' Home quilt (#6) sold for a minimum of $18 each and, as a result, about $5000 was raised in 1882.

Many of the quilts sold at an auction, which might have been held after an ice cream social or a box or pie supper, or sometimes in connection with a bazaar. Clemmie Pugh of Monterey, Tennessee, gave $10 at an auction for the Dresden Plate she helped make, and she said later: "Why, I wouldn't take anything for this quilt. They's so many of them that's dead and gone."[14] I believe that this is the reason why so many of these quilts and their stories are still extant. Several times I heard or read a remark very similar to Clemmie's made by other informants.

Two quilts have amounts of money written on the quilt. One is the "tithing quilt," made about 1860. Each member of the congregation inscribed his or her name around the Oak Leaf applique, and after each name was the sum of money that the individual gave to the minister, 10¢, 15¢ or 25¢. (#2) The other was made by women of the First Christian Church of Adrian, Missouri, in 1911. Each

Fig. 2. Quilt made in 1931 by the women of the First Methodist Church of Bartlesville, Oklahoma. Typical of the 'embroidered wheel' fundraisers of the 1920s and 30s. Photo by Bryan Gammon.

hub contained the name of the person who collected the money for that block and the amount of money collected. (#21)

Some quilts were raffled. However, this method of fundraising was opposed by some churches or some ministers. In the centennial history of the church in Linden, Iowa, cited above, written by Ruth Ketelson, appears the following:

In 1928 in Redfield Rev. Nightengale helped the board decide that the "church would not allow any quilt to be raffled off in the name of any department of the church." Since he was also our minister I doubt if any "raffling" was done here either.[14]

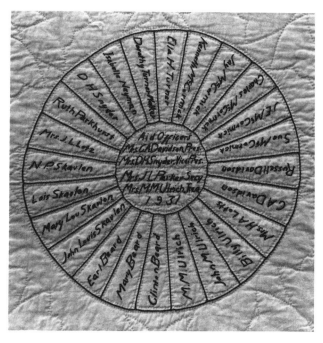

Fig. 3. Detail of Figure 2.

Bonnie Carden recalls the women's experience with a raffle at the Andersonville (Tennessee) Methodist Church. "... we began to get criticism from other members that this was a form of gambling. That was the first and last time we ever raffled a quilt."[15] Of course there were ways of eluding such criticism. One was to give something like a stick of gum in return for the money; if they bought something, they wouldn't be gambling. Another way was to call the money a "donation." Sometimes tickets were handed out in return for a donation, and one such occurrence resulted in my favorite fundraising quilt story. The quilt was probably made in 1944, during World War II. The Women's Missionary Union of a Baptist church in Clark County, Missouri, made a quilt, putting the names of each woman and man then in the Armed Forces in the center of an album block. The only one killed in World War II whose name was on the quilt was Raymond S. Grinstead. In 1946 it was decided to raffle the quilt. During the meeting at which the quilt was raffled, several people announced that they had purchased tickets in Ray's honor. They had put Ray's father's name on the tickets, and perhaps others did the same. At any rate, when the drawing took place, Ray's father's name was on the winning ticket. This quilt, and the story, are still cherished by the Grinstead family. (#48)

What happened to the quilts after the money was raised? Of those not auctioned or raffled, two were given to bishops, one Methodist (#3), and one Church of the Latter Day Saints. (#49) Several were given to the minister of the church in which the quilt was made, and one was given to the woman who collected the most names. (#20) One was bought by the church and presented to the president of the sponsoring organization because she did so much work on it. (#27) At least one person regretted that the quilt her group made had been raffled. She told me that the woman who won the quilt had only one ticket, and then she didn't take care of the quilt and it was worn out long ago. (#47)

In an attempt to determine the areas of the United States were quilts were most often used for fundraising, I compiled a list of all the fundraisers found, almost 100 of them, not just the 49 used in this paper. The findings were inconclusive but interesting. Two were not made in the United States but in Canada, one in Nova Scotia, and one in British Columbia. Most of those found were made in the Midwest, but that is probably because I live in that area, one proof being that I found five in my home county, Garfield County, Oklahoma, although only three of those were made in Oklahoma. Fifteen were made in Oklahoma and two of those were made in the same town, Bartlesville, by two generations of women from the same Methodist church. (#27, #37) Fourteen were made in Kansas, eight in Missouri, eight in Ohio. Altogether quilts were found from twenty states, plus the two from Canada. Few were found that were made west of Oklahoma, Kansas and Nebraska.[16] Determining periods of time in which the making of fundraisers was most popular was equally inconclusive. Although the dates tend to cluster around the 1880s and 1890s and the 1920s and 1930s, I found fundraisers in every decade from the 1850s through the 1960s, except for the 1870s.

Much research remains on this and all aspects of quilt fundraising. Countless women made and sold quilts, or quilted for others to help with their families' finances. Thousands of women's organizations earned money for their churches or other organizations by making quilts and/or quilting and donating the money received, and, indeed, this is still a popular method of fundraising. For about twenty years the Mennonite Central Committee has been holding huge auctions all over the United States, selling quilts and other hand-made articles to raise money for overseas relief. This paper is only an introduction to the subject.

QUILTS, in order of date made:

1. Applique quilt, friendship, made in Akron, Ohio, c. 1850, *America's Quilts and Coverlets*, p. 193.
2. Applique quilt, Oak Leaf, made by members of E. J. Metzler's congregation, probably in Pennsylvania, c. 1860, *America's Quilts and Coverlets*, p. 160.
3. Log Cabin (Straight Furrows), made for a Methodist Episcopal Church bazaar in Missouri in 1866, Missouri Historical Society, St. Louis.
4. Pieced quilt, Sunburst, made by members of Mason Methodist Society, Bethel, Maine, in 1880. Letter from Nancy Halpern, September 12, 1983.
5. Pieced quilt, friendship, made by members of Holy Trinity Church, Yarmouth, Nova Scotia, 1881–82, *Nova Scotia Workbasket*, p. 68.
6. Crazy Quilt, made by various Baptist groups in Kentucky in 1882. *Kentucky Quilts 1880–1900*.
7. Method unknown, wheel quilt, made by Olive Hill (Kansas) Methodist Church in 1884. Letter from Bill Shaklee, January 22, 1983.
8. Crazy Quilt, made by a group of Monroeville, Ohio, women in 1888. *Quilts and Carousels: Folk Art in the Firelands*, p. 22.
9. Embroidered quilt containing names, ads, and a picture of the Garland Street Church, made by the Ladies' Aid Society of the Garland Street Methodist Episcopal Church, Flint, Michigan in 1888. Collection of Sloan Museum, Flint, Michigan. *Flint Journal*, February 18, 1968, page unknown.
10. Pieced and appliqued slumber throw, also painted and embroidered, made by members of Trinity Lutheran Church, Findley, Ohio, in 1890, collection of Smithsonian Institution, Washington, D.C.
11. Embroidered quilt, signature, made in Terre Haute, Indiana, in 1893. *Quilts in America*, p. 241.
12. Crazy Quilt, made by Ladies' Aid Society of the Methodist Episcopal Church, Altoona, Kansas, in 1894. *Lyon County Historical Society Catalog*, Emporia, Kansas, 1983, page unknown.

13. Applique quilt, Spiked Circles, made by members of a Methodist Church in Ohio. Date unknown but the minister to whom it was presented, Charles H. Stocking, born in 1842 and died in 1926. Smithsonian Institution, Washington, D.C.

14. Applique quilt, wheel design, made by a Baptist church in the South in 1898. *Los Angeles Herald Examiner,* December 11, 1983, pp. E3 and E4.

15. Embroidered quilt, State Flowers, made by church women in Oklahoma in the early twentieth century. *A Century of Quilts from the Collection of the Oklahoma Historical Society,* an unpaged catalog, (n.d.)

16. Appliqued quilt, Wheel, made by the women of Asbury Methodist Church near Breckenridge, Oklahoma, in 1902. Telephone interview with the mother of the owner, Marva Shaklee Brix, September 8, 1984.

17. Appliqued quilt Hawaiian design, made by the Ladies' Aid Society of the Mt. Herman Church of North Allen Creek, Americus, Kansas, c. 1900. Phone interview with niece, Dorothy Alexander, of the woman who bought the quilt, September 16, 1984.

18. Pieced quilt, Double T, made by United Evangelical Church women of Montour Falls, New York, in 1902. *Lady's Circle Patchwork Quilts,* No. 17, p. 53.

19. Pieced quilt, Crown of Thorns, variation, made by women of Mission Methodist Church, Mission, British Columbia, 1910. *Three Hundred Years of Canada Quilts,* p. 77.

20. Quilted with names written in indelible ink, spinning wheel design, made by Caughnawaga (New York) Chapter, DAR, in 1911. *Quilts from Montgomery County, New York,* Montgomery County Historical Society, Fort Jackson, N.Y., 1981, quilt number 37.

21. Embroidered quilt, Wagon Wheel, made by the women of the First Christian Church of Adrian, Missouri, in 1911. Letter from Mrs. John Ramsey, granddaughter of Chester Moudy, who won the quilt, September 19, 1983.

22. Embroidered quilt, pattern not indicated, made by women of Alpine School District #153, Tillman County, Oklahoma, in 1914. *Orbit Magazine,* May 8, 1977, p. 22.

23. Crazy Quilt, made by women of Presbyterian Church, Keystone, Nebraska, c. 1919. Letter from Mrs. Willard Wendt, September 23, 1983.

24. Embroidered quilt, pattern not indicated, made by the Ladies' Aid Society of the Keystone (Nebraska) Methodist Church, c. 1915. Letter from Mrs. Willard Wendt, September 23, 1983.

25. Applique quilt, Wheel, made by women of Bartlesville (Oklahoma) Methodist Church in 1915. Interview with Ruth Montgomery, September 7, 1984.

26. Embroidered quilt, circular pattern, made by Ladies' Aid Society of the Methodist Church (Shamburg, Iowa), in 1924. Letter from present owners, Forest and Glola Richardson, son and daughter-in-law of Arthur Richardson, who purchased the quilt originally, September 15, 1984.

27. Pieced quilt, Nine Patch, variation, made by "The Calendar," a women's group of the Plymouth Congregational Church, Lawrence, Kansas, c. 1920. *The Lawrence Journal World*, 1977, page unknown.

28. Pieced quilt, Streak of Lightning, made by Ladies' Aid society of Linden (Iowa) Methodist Church in the 1920s. *Centennial 1882–1982*, p. 8.

29. Pieced quilt, friendship, made by Ladies' Aid Society of the Methodist Church, Aulne, Kansas, c. 1924. Interview with present owner, Mrs. Ed Klein, daughter of the woman who won the quilt, July 28, 1973.

30. Pieced quilt, Double Irish Chain, made by the women of Rupe's Grove Church, Atchinson County, Missouri, in 1923. Letter from present owner, Mrs. Henry L. Knock, September 23, 1983.

31. Embroidered quilt, Friendship Ring, made by the ladies of the Second Baptist Church of Williamston, South Carolina, in 1923. South Carolina History Project, Laurel Horton, Guest Curator, McKissick Museums.

32. Applique quilt, Wheel, made by Baptist women's group near Colby, Kansas, in 1924. Telephone conversation with Enola Gish, August 23, 1963.

33. Embroidered quilt, Friendship Ring, made by ladies of Tabernacle Baptist Church, Pelzer, South Carolina, in 1927. South Carolina Quilt History Project, Laurel Horton, Guest Curator, McKissick Museums.

34. Crazy Quilt, made by LGAR, Garfield Circle #22, Emporia, Kansas, in 1928. *Lyon County Historical Society Catalog*, Emporia, Kansas, 1983, (unpaged).

35. Embroidered quilt, Friendship Ring, made by Division 10, Central Christian Church, Enid, Oklahoma, in 1929. Interview with present owners, Mr. and Mrs. James Henderson, son and daughter-in-law of original owner, July 10, 1983.

36. Pieced quilt, Single Irish Chain, made by Town Circle, First Congregational Church, Austinburg, Ohio, in 1930, *Quilts and Carousels*, p. 22.

37. Embroidered quilt, Wheel, made by women of First Methodist Church, Bartlesville, Oklahoma, 1931. Interview with Mary Lou Holliman, daughter of original owner, September 7, 1984.

38. Appliqued and pieced quilt, Dresden Plate, made by a church in Rowan County, North Carolina in the late 1930s. Letter from Laurel Horton, June 28, 1984.

39. Embroidered quilt, friendship, made by members of Methodist Church, Baldwin, Kansas, in 1939. *Kansas Quilt Symposium 1978*, catalog, Lawrence, Kansas, p. 77.
40. Appliqued and pieced quilt, Church Quilt, made by women of a Baptist church in Tennessee in 1935. *A People and Their Quilts*, p. 95.
41. Pieced quilt, friendship, made by Women's Missionary Society of the First Methodist Church, Hollister, Oklahoma, in the 1930s. *Orbit Magazine*, May 8, 1977, p. 23.
42. Pieced and appliqued quilt, friendship, made by the women of the Methodist Church in Keefer, Oklahoma, in the 1930s. *Nimble Needle Treasures*, Vol. 7, No. 2, 1975, p. 28.
43. Appliqued quilt, Refrigerator Quilt, made by women of Trinity Evangelical Church, Kansas City, Kansas, in 1935 and 1936. Letter from present owner, Lois Brunner, December 19, 1983.
44. Pieced quilt, I T or It, made by a senior class at Homestead, Oklahoma, High School in early 1930s. Interview with Ann Warkentin, September 8, 1984.
45. Appliqued quilt, Sunflower, made by women of Congregational Church, Drummond, Oklahoma, c. 1940. Interview with several of the church members.
46. Appliqued quilt, original flower, made by women of Furman Baptist Church, Furman, South Carolina, in 1941. South Carolina Quilt Project, letter from Laurel Horton, Guest Curator, McKissick Museums.
47. Pattern unknown, made by Golden Circle Club, Ashley Community, Grant County, Oklahoma, c. 1943. Interview with one of the club members.
48. Pieced quilt, album block, made by the Women's Missionary Union of a Baptist Church in Clark County, Missouri, c. 1944. Letter from Rosie Grinstead, September 14, 1984.
49. Embroidered quilt, Beehive and Seagull, made for Bishop Earl W. Walker by members of a ward of the Church of the Latter Day Saints. *Utah Folk Art*, B.Y.U. Press (n.d.).

Notes and References:

1. Patsy and Myron Orlofsky, *Quilts in America*, (New York: McGraw Hill, 1974), p. 241.
2. Carleton Safford and Robert Bishop, *America's Quilts and Coverlets*, (New York: Weathervane Books, 1974), p. 161 and p. 193.
3. Mary Conroy, *Three Hundred Years of Canadian Quilts*, (Toronto: Griffin House, 1976), pp. 60-61, 84, 95, and 77.
4. John Rice Irwin, *A People and Their Quilts*, (Exton, Pennsylvania: Schiffer, 1983), pp. 95, 13316, 82, 142, 193.
5. John Finley and Jonathan Holstein, *Kentucky Quilts 1800-1900*, (Louisville: Kentucky Quilt Project, Inc., 1982), pp. 60-63.
6. Ricky Clark, *Quilts and Carousels: Folk Art in the Firelands*, (Oberlin, Ohio: FAVA, 1983, p. 22.
7. Marlene Davis, Joan Creelman, *et. al.*, *Nova Scotia Workbasket*, (Halifax: Nova Scotia Museum, 1976), p. 68.
8. Nancy J. Rowley, "Red Cross Quilts for the Great War," *Uncoverings 1982*, (Mill Valley, California: American Quilt Study Group, 1983), pp. 43-51.
9. *Holton* (Kansas) *Recorder*, July, 1927, page unknown.
10. When this paper was read at the 1984 AQSG Seminar, Virginia Gunn, explained in answer to a question, that so many of these quilts used red because it was the color most sure to be colorfast.
11. Letter from Mary Barton, received May 16, 1984.
12. Ruth Ketelson, *Centennial 1882-1982*, Linden, Iowa, 1982, unpublished manuscript, p. 8.
13. Conroy. p. 77.
14. Irwin, p. 95.
15. Ketelson.
16. Since presenting this paper I have received information about fundraising quilts in Colorado, Pennsylvania, California, and Missouri. I would also refer the reader to Suzanne Yabsley, *Texas Quilts, Texas Women*, (College Station, Texas: Texas A. and M. University Press), pp. 28, 72 and 85.

Quiltmaking Traditions in South Carolina

Laurel Horton

The quiltmaking traditions of a particular geographic area are best understood when examined in the context of the area's history. Human activities generally reflect the influences of geographic features such as mountains or rivers, agricultural economy, the ethnic background of its inhabitants, as well as specific historical events such as wars and depressions.

Within South Carolina, the smallest Southeastern state, there are three recognizable geographic regions: the flat, low-lying *Coastal Plain*, the pine tree covered central *Sandhills* which represent the dunes of an earlier east coast, and the higher, red clay hills of the *Piedmont*, rimmed by the southeastern edge of the Blue Ridge Mountains. The physical features of these three regions influenced their settlement and development in different ways, which in turn produced a variety of quiltmaking traditions.

In 1983, McKissick Museum at the University of South Carolina and the South Carolina State Museum jointly received a grant from the National Endowment for the Arts Folk Arts Program to survey and examine quiltmaking traditions in the three geographical regions. The survey was designed to sample quilts in a representative county in each region: Charleston in the Coastal Plain, Richland in the Sandhills and Greenville in the Piedmont.

During the six months of the survey period the project held Quilt History Days in community centers within the three counties. Four to seven Quilt History Days were held in each area. Prior to these days the project staff held an orientation workshop to train community people to help gather the data. On the Quilt History Days, volunteers interviewed the owners using a two-page questionnaire while the quilts were photographed and examined. The resulting

Laurel Horton: 302 E. South Third St, Seneca, SC 29678

data for over 1300 quilts are housed at McKissick Museum for use by interested researchers. Twenty quilts identified in the survey formed the traveling exhibition "Social Fabric: South Carolina's Traditional Quilts," touring during 1984–1986. The project staff also prepared a book of essays and photographs called *Social Fabric* which includes a catalog of the exhibition.

NEA Folk Arts funded the project for a second year in 1984–85 to continue the survey in six additional counties. The resulting data will add to the general findings and allow staff to examine more subtle variations in quilt styles and techniques in the state. Future plans include designing a package so that small museums, historical societies, and quilt guilds in other parts of South Carolina could hold quilt surveys in conjunction with McKissick and the State Museum. Important considerations include maintaining the quality of the photographs and data, establishing a system by which both the survey and maintenance of the data can be a continuing process, and encouraging groups to sponsor the survey in their own areas.

Following the survey phase in 1984, the project staff studied the slides and data looking for broad characteristics in historical and geographical distribution. Some of the resulting conclusions were predictable, others surprising. As these data are examined more thoroughly, other more subtle trends will appear and generalizations will break down into more complex categories. The additional data from succeeding projects will enhance the value of the basic collection. What follows is a general discussion of historical and geographical variations in South Carolina quiltmaking as revealed by an analysis of the first year's survey.

General trends in the quiltmaking traditions of the three geographic regions reflect the distinct history and development of each area. Charleston was the largest city and primary port in the pre-Civil War South. As the center of trade and commerce for the Carolinas and Georgia, Charleston served as the funnel for the export of agricultural and forest products and the importation of finished goods, including textiles. Early rice plantations and the use of slave labor contributed to the success of many planters, and shops and businesses developed in Charleston to meet the needs of the wealthy inhabitants. The early bedcovers in Charleston area homes

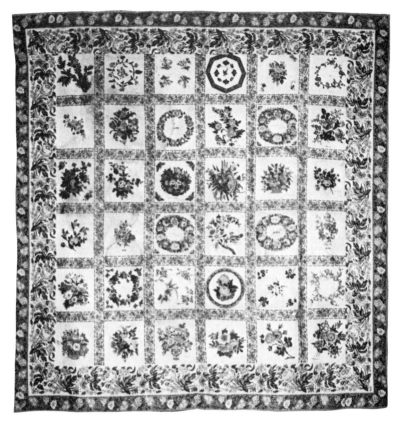

Fig. 1. Chintz applique album quilt, Charleston vicinity, made for former S.C. Governor James H. Hammond 1846–48. 102" x 100"

were European, including wool blankets from England and whole-cloth quilts from southern France.[1] Household inventories for Colonial Charleston list an impressive array of fine imported furnishings.[2] Gradually Charleston area residents turned to locally produced textiles to supply some of their needs for clothing and bedcovers. Experimental textile mills in the Coastal Plain produced some goods for local consumption, and there is evidence that some large planters set up weaving operations to make coarse fabrics for slave clothing and bedding.[3]

In spite of trends toward the use of locally produced textiles, antebellum Charlestonians continued to import many commodities and to be influenced by European styles. Nineteenth century quilts from Charleston fall into a number of discrete historical periods, reflecting the changing fads and fashions of the times. The earliest of the styles appears to be white whole-cloth quilts made from the late eighteenth century to about 1820 modelled after imported Marseilles quilts and English stuffed quilts. Generally these are quilted, stuffed, and corded, in a framed center style in motifs of wreaths and vines. While beautifully ornamented they are usually not as complex as their European antecedents.

In the early nineteenth century white quilts were supplanted in Charleston by another European quilt type. Chintz applique quilts, also in a framed center style, appeared in profusion. "Chintz" describes a type of printed fabric originally developed in India. The fabric, techniques and arrangements in these quilts are mostly of English origin. The majority of extant chintz framed center quilts from the Charleston area appear to be from the period of 1830–1850. By this time fabric manufacturers were producing furnishing fabrics especially adaptable for use in quilts, both as center motifs and stripes to be cut apart for borders. The same fabrics are often found in several different quilts, suggesting that some prints may have been especially favored for quilts. Two popular prints used in the centers of several floral applique quilts are the "bouquet of flowers with scrollwork border" and the "trophy of arms."[4]

Friendship quilts, which combine blocks by different contributors were fashionable in the eastern United States in the 1840s and 50s. The best known of this style are attributed to the Baltimore area and contain fabrics with small figured prints.[5] Friendship quilts were very popular within the busy social network of Charleston residents. Almost invariably they used their favored chintz fabrics for these group projects. A chintz applique friendship quilt made by women in the Charleston area was presented to former Governor James H. Hammond in 1848.[6] New brides and other individuals received similar quilts from groups of friends.

In the 1850s, another European style took precedence among fashionable Charleston quiltmakers. During this decade *Godey's* and other American ladies' magazines printed a series of articles on English template piecing.[7] In this technique small templates, usually in the shape of hexagons or diamonds, are cut from paper, then are covered by a somewhat larger piece of fabric and the edges turned

Fig. 2. Template pieced cotton quilt top, Charleston, c. 1875. 96" x 88"

under and basted. The individual pieces are whip stitched together to form a quilt top. A number of template pieced hexagon quilts made in Charleston survive. Additionally, because the technique is intricate and time-consuming, many unfinished tops remain, some still containing paper templates. While the instructors in *Godey's* suggested silk as the appropriate fabric for this work, Charlestonians first adapted the technique to their favored cotton chintzes. As silks, especially remnants from northern companies[8] became more available, silk pieced quilts made their appearance.

In the period 1800–1900 Charlestonians like their sisters elsewhere turned to making crazy quilts. Constructed in blocks of odd-shaped pieces of silks and velvets, and decorated with a variety of ornamental embroidery stitches, crazy quilts represented a widespread fashion apparently of American origin.[9] Many Charleston area crazy quilts survive, and most are very similar to crazy quilts made elsewhere in the country.

Fig. 3. Whig's Defeat, *pieced and appliqued quilt made by Sarah Adeline Stewart, Greenville County, c. 1870. 91" x 84"*

Nineteenth century quilts from Charleston divide neatly into time periods marked by changing fashions. However, quilts made in other parts of the state during the same periods reflect trends which ebbed and flowed more gradually. In the Piedmont the prevailing lifestyle was rural and agricultural rather than urban and commercial. The area forming the present Greenville County was part of the Cherokee nation until 1777, by which time Charleston was a well established and influential city. After the area was acquired from the Indians by treaty, settlers flocked to the fertile rolling hills. Many were of Scotch-Irish origin who followed a trail of migration from Pennsylvania through Virginia and North Carolina. Others entered the country through Charleston and still others left their homes in the coastal settlements in search of cheaper land.

Fig. 4. Pineapple *made by Ann Smith, Richland County, c. 1880. 74" x 73"*

Many early Piedmont farmers took large holdings, owned slaves, and established successful farms. They raised a variety of agricultural products, both for their own use and to trade for commercial wares. The wealth of these families was measured in land, livestock, crops, and tools rather than by cash assets and bank accounts. Cash and banks were scarce in the back country, and most families relied on barter locally. Household inventories list an impressive array of farm equipment and household implements.[10]

Bedcovers, both in inventories and in the survey, reflect the greater use of local materials over imported textiles. Suviving bedcovers produced in the Piedmont in the first half of the 19th century included primarily overshot woven coverlets and various forms of white-work. White whole-cloth quilts and bedspreads made in this area included a variety of techniques. Some are stuffed and corded, some are candlewick, others are white-on-white embroidery. All of those surveyed are designed in a framed center style and feature floral motifs, wreathes, and such elements as grape clusters and pineapples. While they display designs of moderate complexity, those that are quilted do not show the elaborate close rows of stitching that appear on earlier English and French whole-cloth quilts.

The conclusion drawn from the sample is that Piedmont quilt-makers continued to make whole-cloth white quilts for their fine bedcovers long after Charleston residents had dropped the style in favor of the chintz applique style. Because of the necessity of trading their agricultural and forest products in Charleston and other cities, Piedmont residents would have been aware of the new fashions; however, being apart from that society, they were less affected by the need for "keeping up with the Joneses." While many could have afforded to use some of their barter credit for imported chintzes, such choices were apparently not of high priority.

A second influence contributing to the extended popularity of white quilts centered in the existence of many experiments in cotton spinning mills in the Piedmont.[11] Several dozen were attempted during the early decades of the nineteenth century. While most factories did not survive for very long, they converted raw cotton into a yarn that was strong enough to use for warp threads on the looms of local home weavers. This new abundance gave area quiltmakers a wider range of home-woven products, including the white cotton sheeting which forms the basis of all the white work techniques.

During the 1850s Piedmont quiltmakers also made friendship quilts, yet they rarely used the chintzes favored in Charleston. Almost invariably their friendship quilts contain applique blocks combining solid colors. Unlike the more elaborate Baltimore style, typical individual block design in Piedmont friendship quilts appear to have been drawn from the regular repertoire of applique quilt patterns, including local variations on rose, tulip, and pineapple designs.

While few Piedmont quiltmakers made chintz quilts during the early 19th century, they seem to have retained the idea that these printed florals were desirable for quilts. By the time inexpensive roller-printed chintzes became available to them in mid-century however, quilt styles had changed. Exacting pieced and appliqued patterns calling for sharp contrasts replaced the use of pictorial cutouts, and the new patterns required small figured calicoes and solid colors. Quiltmakers therefore satisfied their desire for chintz by using whole strips of it as borders. The design and colors of these printed borders often have little or no relation to the colors or patterns in the body of the quilt.[12]

During the second half of the nineteenth century, while Charleston quiltmakers were keeping up the current crazy quilt and English template piecing styles, Piedmont seamstresses generally ignored these new techniques and explored a wide range of intricate pieced and appliqued patterns. Rocky Mountain Road[13] is an example of a pattern which was very popular in the Piedmont between about 1875 and 1900. The comparatively large number of quilts and unquilted tops of this pattern from an area of about five counties suggests that this intricate pieced pattern enjoyed a local reputation as a mark of accomplishment among quiltmakers. Perhaps the competition among needleworkers in the Upstate focused on traditional technical skills in this area in this decade when Charleston women were outdoing each other making template and crazy quilts.

The survey identified no template pieced quilts from the Piedmont. The earliest crazy quilt is dated 1890 and is visually distinctive from those made in Charleston at the same time. The Greenville County crazy quilt is primarily of wool, the embroidery joining the blocks is a simple briar stitch rather than a wide range of elaborate stitches, and the floral transfers are primarily simple and straightforward rather than fanciful. Other Piedmont quiltmakers gradually included the crazy quilt in their bag of tricks but they adapted the original decorative function to a utilitarian one. Early twentieth century Piedmont crazy quilts were made of either cotton or wool scraps (in large pieces) lapped together with a simple briar stitch with little or no additional decoration. What began as purely decorative technique was adapted and simplified to suit the more practical tastes of the Piedmont.

The 1870s and 1880s in the Piedmont saw the rapid development of the local textile industry. This activity influenced quiltmakers in several ways. Rural families moved into mill villages and traded their barter economy for one of cash and scrip. The textile mills produced a new array of inexpensive cottons prized by quiltmakers whether living in the villages, in other towns, or in the country. The mills also produced as by-products damaged, misprinted, or surplus remnants, which thrifty quiltmakers acquired at little cost. One result of these occurrences is an explosion of scrap quilts beginning in the last two decades of the nineteenth century. In addition to fine quilts of two or three colors the new scrap quilts developed, first as variations in which one or two segments of a pattern shift while the rest remains constant. Eventually, by 1900, scrap quilts exhibited more random application of color and fabric. In this area the widespread use of scraps of inexpensive fabric in quilts appears to coincide with their local production and availability.

Richland County, located in the central Sandhills or Midlands presents a blending of the Coastal and Piedmont quiltmaking traditions. The area was settled during the mid-1800s by German, Scotch-Irish, and English immigrants and by Charlestonians seeking new opportunities. In 1786, the legislature selected a site on the Congaree River in the center of the state, for the new capital to be called Columbia. Thus a new planned city, with an established gentry and their accoutrements, was developed in the middle of the rural back country. Evidence suggests that both fashionable urban and conservative rural quiltmaking styles existed side by side in Richland County. Unfortunately, in February 1865, the major portion of downtown Columbia and its homes were destroyed in a fire during the city's occupation by Sherman's troops. Very few antebellum quilts from Columbia survived compared with other parts of the state. Late nineteenth century Midlands quilts include crazy quilts influenced by Charleston styles, intricate pieced and applique patterns resembling fine Piedmont quilts and scrap quilts resulting from the existence of local textile mills.

By the early 1900s South Carolinians, responding to a growing national trend toward manufactured goods, generally preferred purchased spreads on their beds to fancy homemade quilts. However, many women continued to take advantage of inexpensive local materials and made scrap quilts for everyday use and for personal satisfaction. Made during a time when quiltmaking followed practical considerations rather than popular formulas, these quilts are catalogs of the kinds of fabrics used by home sewers for family clothing. They generally contained pieces of various stripes, plaids, and solids rather than the small-figured prints of the 19th century and, later, the 1930s.

By the late 1920s and 1930s women who had grown up with blankets and spreads from Sears, Roebuck and Company took up quiltmaking. The Great Depression often receives credit for this

Fig. 5. String quilt, made by Mary Patterson Coster, Traveler's Rest, Greenville County, c. 1900. 71" x 69"

upsurge in quilting activity, but the reasons are more complex. Perhaps the post-World War I emphasis on modernism, characterized by automobile and "flapper" dress, was answered by the commemoration of values associated with earlier times. In an article in the women's pages of the Progressive Farmer, December 31, 1927, the editor introduces an article titled "Grandmother's Quilts Becoming Popular Again" with the following statement: "At no time in American history has there been more ardent love for old houses, old furniture, old songs, and old quilts."[14]

Pattern companies, popular magazines, and quilt books during the early twentieth century emphasize the nostalgic and romantic aspects of early American life generally and quilts specifically.

Many South Carolina quiltmakers took advantage of the variety of new and old patterns offered through syndicated pattern columns in their local newspapers in the late 1920s and 1930s. Generally women seem to have selected special new patterns and new fabrics for their "best" quilts and to have made utility quilts in more traditional patterns and with scraps. Thus an old system of individual

Fig. 6. Star, *or* Sunflower *made by Martha D. Richardson, James Island, Charleston County, 1977. 74" x 67"*

and local pattern transmission and a new system of mass media inspirations existed happily side by side. The juxtaposition of these two methods continued among traditional quiltmakers at least until the 1970s.

One special group of contemporary quilts, those made by Afro-American quiltmakers, are of particular interest. Many of these quilts represent a highly distinctive aesthetic tradition maintained through the years in black communities in spite of slavery, social workers and other forms of intervention. While a large number of black quiltmakers use the same patterns as their white neighbors, many other Afro-American quilts are characterized by bold, often assymetrical arrangements, large design elements, bright colors often in dynamic contrasts, and multiplicity of pattern (having more than one theme). These quilts are sometimes conceptualized and constructed in strips running the length of the quilts rather than in blocks. The intuition and innovation of Afro-American

4

quilt design parallels the same characteristics in sacred and secular music and other oral traditions.[15]

The sea islands along the coast near Charleston have been the site for the study of African retentions in Afro-American life generally, and the quilts and other folk art made there have been the subject of much attention in recent years. The interaction between black and white quiltmakers, the influence on black quilt styles by white missionaries encouraging the making of quilts to sell to whites, and the interplay between individual expression and traditional design inspiration are among the complex subjects for future research.

While earlier writers have largely ignored Southern quiltmaking or have generalized that Southern quilts were "almost invariably artistic creations little handicapped by economic conditions,"[16] preliminary analysis of the survey results reveals a more complex picture. Within the boundaries of a single small southern state are found examples of a multiplicity of traditions. These general quiltmaking traditions can be mapped out geographically and historically to reflect the influences of settlement history, agricultural economy, ethnic background, social organization and other cultural factors. The complex interaction of such influences must be studied in order to truly document and understand the context of quilts surveyed in a given area.

Notes and References:

1. Sally Garoutte, "Marseilles Quilts and their Woven Offspring," *Uncoverings 1982* (Mill Valley, CA: American Quilt Study Group), pp. 115–134.
2. Charleston County Probate Inventories; Department of Archives and History, Columbia, SC.
3. Theresa Singleton, "Textiles in South Carolina," in *Social Fabric: South Carolina's Traditional Quilts* (Columbia, SC: McKissick Museum, 1985).

4. Florence Montgomery, *Printed Textiles*, A Winterthur Book (New York: Viking, 1970), p. 356, figs. 420 and 421.
5. Dena Katzenberg, *Baltimore Album Quilts* (Baltimore: Baltimore Museum of Art, 1981).
6. Chintz applique friendship quilt, made by various Charleston area residents. In collection of Jane Hammond Jervey.
7. Virginia Gunn, "Victorian Silk Template Patchwork in American Periodicals, 1850–1875;" *Uncoverings 1983*, (Mill Valley, CA: American Quilt Study Group), pp. 9–25.
8. Katy Christopherson, "19th Century Craze for Crazy Quilts," *Quilter's Journal* (Spring 1978), p. 9.
9. Penny McMorris, *Crazy Quilts* (New York: E.P. Dutton, 1984).
10. Greenville County Probate Records. Department of Archives and History, Columbia, SC.
11. Ernest Lander, *The Textile Industry in Antebellum South Carolina* (Baton Rouge: Louisiana State University Press, 1969).
12. Pieced and appliqued quilt, Whig's Defeat, made by Sarah Adeline Stewart, c. 1875, Fountain Inn (Greenville County) SC. Collection of Joyce Pendarvis.
13. Barbara Brackman, *An Encyclopedia of Pieced Quilt Patterns*, v. 1–8 (Lawrence, KS: Prairie Flower Publishing, 1979–83), #1077. This pattern was described by twentieth century writers as "New York Beauty."
14. Erma Kirkpatrick, "Quilts in the Progressive Farmer, 1886–1935," unpublished research, 1984.
15. John Vlach, *The Afro-American Tradition in Decorative Arts* (Cleveland Museum of Art, 1978); Maude Wahlman and Ella King Torrey, *Ten Afro-American Quilters* (Center for the Study of Southern Culture, 1983); Cuesta Benberry, "Afro-American Women and Quilts," *Uncoverings 1980* (Mill Valley, CA: American Quilt Study Group), pp. 64–67.
16. Ruth Finley, *Old Patchwork Quilts* (Newton Centre, MA: Branford, 1929), p. 39–40; Lilian Baker Carlisle, *Pieced Work and Applique Quilts at the Shelburne Museum* (Shelburne, VT: The Shelburne Museum, 1957), p. 73.

Bibliography

Benberry, Cuesta. "Afro-American Women and Quilts," in *Uncoverings 1980*, Mill Valley, CA: American Quilt Study Group, 1981, pp. 64–67.

Bridenbaugh, Carol. *Myths and Realities: Societies of the Colonial South.* Baton Rouge: Louisiana State University Press, 1952.

Carawan, Guy, and Carawan, Candie. *Ain't You Got a Right to the Tree of Life? The People of Johns Island, South Carolina.* New York: Simon and Schuster, 1966.

Christoperson, Kathryn D. "19th Century Craze for Crazy Quilts." *Quilter's Journal* (Spring 1978), p. 9.

Garoutte, Sally. "Early Colonial Quilts in a Bedding Context," in *Uncoverings 1980*. Mill Valley, CA: American Quilt Study Group, 1981, pp. 18–27.

Garoutte, Sally. "Marseilles Quilts and Their Woven Offspring," in *Uncoverings 1982*. Mill Valley, CA: American Quilt Study Group, 1983, pp. 115–135.

Gunn, Virginia. "Victorian Silk Template Patchwork in American Periodicals, 1850–1875," in *Uncoverings 1983*. Mill Valley, CA: American Quilt Study Group, 1984, pp. 9–25.

Horton, Laurel. *Economic Influences on German and Scotch-Irish Quilts in Antebellum Rowan County, North Carolina.* Thesis. Chapel Hill: University of North Carolina, 1979.

Lander, Ernest. *The Textile Industry in Antebellum South Carolina.* Baton Rouge, LA: Louisiana State University Press, 1969.

McMorris, Penny. *Crazy Quilts.* New York: E.P. Dutton, 1984.

Meyer, Suellen. "Design Characteristics of Missouri-German Quilts," forthcoming in *Uncoverings 1984*. Mill Valley, CA: American Quilt Study Group, 1985.

Michie, Audrey. "Charleston Textile Imports, 1738–1742." *Journal of Early Southern Decorative Arts* 8 (1): pp. 20–39.

Montgomery, Florence M. *Printed Textiles: English and American Cottons and Linens 1700–1850.* A Winterthur Book. New York: The Viking Press, 1970. *Textiles in America.* New York: W.W. Norton and Co., 1984.

A Family of Texas Quilters and Their Work

Sandra M. Todaro

The Texas hill country bears little resemblance to the popular idea of Texas. Unlike the flat dry plains of west Texas, or the low-lying humid lands in south Texas, the hill country in east Texas is a land of pine forests, gently rolling hills and spring-fed streams. Farms rather than cattle ranches predominate. In the 1800s and early 1900s cotton was the principal cash crop grown on these farms.

First settled in the 1830s, the hill country has a strong German background. Towns such as New Braunfels and Fredericksburg bear witness to the German influence. Neches in Anderson County, Kerrville in Kerr County, and Jacksonville in Cherokee County are all within this area.[1]

In March 1983, I found a lovely old Blazing Star quilt in a shop in Dallas. The quilt seemed to call to me, so I paid the price and took it home. The shop owner mentioned that she had several other quilts from the same family for sale.

Later, after I purchased two more quilts from this family group, the shop owner gave me the name and address of the lady who had placed the quilts on consignment. Wanting to know more about the women who had made these quilts, I contacted the lady who was selling them, Mrs. Hilda Palmer of Kerrville, Texas.

Mrs. Palmer told me she had several more quilts at her home. The responsibility for so many quilts was more than she wanted; so, keeping the ones dearest to her mother, she placed the others up for sale. Mrs. Palmer had made only two quilts in her life, one a baby quilt for her daughters; and didn't consider herself a quilter.

This study came about when something very interesting in the stitching of one of the quilts was revealed by the sun as the back of the quilt was turned to the light. There in the stitchwork was the

Sandra M. Todaro: 9608 N. Charlotte, Kansas City, MO 64155

word *"Mollie,"* and the date *"1871."* There, as her living legacy, was a signature of a young woman, reaching across the years. One could sense the pride Mollie must have experienced as she put her name on her handiwork.

According to Mrs. Palmer, the women represented by these quilts were: her mother, grandmother, great-grandmother, great-aunt, and great-great-aunt. It is unusual that so many quilts, made by members of one family, still remained after such a long time.

There are sixteen quilts in the family group. They were made over a span of 70 years by five women. Four of these women were related by blood, the fifth by marriage.[2]

In general, the quilts are in very good condition and represent a variety of patterns. There are three applique quilts, ten pieced quilts and three in which the designs are both pieced and appliqued.

The first of the five women was Mary Jonathan "Mollie" McDow, born 1842 in Adairsville, Georgia, a small town northwest of Atlanta. She married Guilford McReynolds, a Confederate veteran, in 1872 and moved to Texas in 1875.[3] They settled in Neches where Guilford went into the lumber business. They also farmed and raised poultry, eventually developing a new breed of chicken. Guilford also published a poultry magazine.[4]

Mollie died, childless, in 1897 and is buried in the old Neches City Cemetery.[5]

Four of the quilts in the group were her work; a green and brown Tulip, which is the one she signed; the Feathered Star; the Basket; and the Blazing Star.

After Mollie's death at 55, Guilford remarried, put his first wife's quilts away and used them very little, if at all. There were no children from Guilford's second marriage either; so upon his death and that of his second wife, the quilts became the property of Mary Abram "Abbie" Fuller, Guilford's niece and the fifth child of his sister, Tennessee Jane McReynolds Fuller.[6]

Tennie Jane, as she was called, was born in Alabama in 1847. In 1869 she married Abram J. Fuller. They, too, moved to Texas in 1875 and settled in Neches. Abram died in 1878, leaving Tennie Jane with four small children and pregnant with a fifth baby. To support herself and her children she took over the management of the farm and ran it, as well as the local cotton gin, in an age when few women were actively involved in business. Tennie Jane died in

*Fig. 1. Mary Jonathan "Mollie"
McDow McReynolds (1842–1897)*

*Fig. 2. Tennessee Jane McReynolds
Fuller (1847–1898)*

*Fig. 3. Mattie Fuller Andrews
(1871–1950)*

*Fig. 4. Vada Andrews Prather
(1894–1977)*

1898 and is buried in the Neches City Cemetery. Before she died,
Tennie Jane produced several quilts, among them a greenish-brown
and red Tulip, the Mexican Rose, and the Chimney Sweep.

Two of Tennie Jane's daughters are represented in the collection
as well.

Mattie Fuller, Tennie Jane's daughter and Mrs. Palmer's grandmother, was born in Alabama in 1871, but grew up in Neches. She
married Terrell Graves Andrews in Neches in 1893, lived in Jacksonville, Texas most of her life and died in Dallas in 1950.[7] She made

the Anna's Irish Tulip, the Double Wedding Ring and the Dutch Doll.

Mattie's sister, Mary Abram or Abbie, was the child born to Tennie Jane four months after her husband's death. In memory of her husband she named the little girl Mary Abram and called her "Abbie."[8] Abbie was something of a family pet and stayed at home with her mother, marrying only after her mother's death. She moved to Palestine, Texas, county seat of Anderson County, and in 1916, married John Blanton of Neches. They moved to Dallas where she was living at the time of her death in 1962. Since she had no children, all the quilts in her possession passed on to her niece, Vada, the daughter of Mattie Fuller Andrews.[9] Abbie made the pink and green Goose Tracks and the Texas Tears.

Vada Andrews, Hilda Palmer's mother, was born in Jacksonville, Texas in 1894. She married the Reverend Hugh Bryant Prather of Weatherford, Texas in April, 1912.[10] The Friendship quilt was a wedding present to them from his family and contains the names of several of his relatives.

Vada died in Dallas in 1977. According to Mrs. Palmer, her mother made only a few quilts, turning instead to crochet and tatting as a creative outlet. The last quilt Vada made was the Grandmother's Flower Garden completed in 1938. Her other quilts are the Dresden Plate and Fruit Basket. The latter was made from a Ruby McKim pattern she ordered by mail in the late 1920s or early 30s.

THE QUILTS

1. Blazing Star—made by Mollie McReynolds, ca. 1870s.
   Total size: 75" by 90". Star size: 14½". Border: 8½". Border block: 2¼".
   This quilt is hand pieced of forest green, gold, reddish brown and white cotton solids. There are twenty stars set in rows of four across and five down. The border is four rows deep in a checkerboard pattern of forest green and white. The quilt shows attention to detail in the piecing and quilting. The hand quilting is fine, with each diamond in the star's outline quilted. There is fine cross-hatch, or Xs, in the border block. The quilt is bound in a brown, hand-sewn binding. This binding is somewhat frayed. The corners of the quilt are rounded. The quilt

back is a red and white plaid fabric. It also has a very thin cotton batting. Unfortunately, the quilt has several stains, although it shows no evidence of hard use. The fabric of the back is very fragile.

2. Baskets, made by Mollie McReynolds, ca. 1870s or 80s.
Total size: 66″ by 76″. Block size: 8¾″.
Hand pieced and quilted of assorted cotton calicoes, this quilt is composed of thirty basket blocks and twenty solid blocks. The baskets are set within white squares which are set on point and alternate with squares of a reddish-pink print. The quilting is done in an all-over waves pattern. This is also known as fan or shell quilting in other parts of the country. There is no evidence of wear and no obvious fabric deterioration. The baskets are of different cotton solids, plaids and prints in colors of dark blue, gold, maroon, tan, red, brown and light blue. The gold is the same fabric used in the Blazing Star. A blue print from the Chimney Sweep appears in one basket, evidence of trading of these fabics among family members.

3. Tulip, bearing the signature in stitching: "Mollie 1871."
Total size: 66″ by 85″. Block size: 17½″. Inner sash: 2″. Outer sash: 3″.
This quilt is composed of green figured calico, a brown cotton solid, (probably red once) and white. There are twelve blocks set three across and four down. The quilting is done in the waves pattern. The quilt is bound in a black and tan print. This binding is not original. The original binding underneath is the green calico used in the tulips. The quilt shows severe fabric deterioration on the back and has several rips around the edges where hands have pulled through the quilt. This quilt is almost identical to the Tulip made about the same time by Tennie Jane Fuller, Mollie's sister-in-law.

4. Feathered Star, made by Mollie McReynolds, ca. 1800s–90s.
Total size: 76″ by 94″. Block size: 18″. Sashes: 4½″. Side Borders: 6½″. Top and bottom borders: 4½″.
This quilt is hand pieced in a variety of cotton prints, plaids and solids. Several prints used in this quilt also appear in the Baskets quilt and Chimney Sweep. The borders and sashes are a red and black cotton print. There are eight khaki and four gray block backgrounds. The quilt contains a great deal of red, navy

Fig. 5. Tulip, made by "Mollie" McDow McReynolds, date inscribed in quilting, "1871."

and mustard yellow prints. The tan binding is machine sewn. The corners are rounded. The quilting is in the waves pattern, but the design of the rows are grouped in lines of three, with a one inch space between groupings. The quilt is in very good condition, with no evidence of hard wear.

5. Chimney Sweep, made by Tennie Jane Fuller, ca. 1870s–80s. Total size: 68″ by 78″. Block size: 9½″ and 10½″. Sashes: 2¾″. Top and bottom borders: 5⅞″. Side borders 8¾″. This small hand pieced and quilted piece is made of various

Fig. 6. *Chimney Sweep*, made by Tennessee Jane Fuller, ca. 1870–1880.

shades of blue prints with one green print block, one khaki solid block and two tan print blocks mixed in. The twenty blocks are cotton prints with muslin centers. The quilting is done in the waves design. This quilt, too, is in excellent condition with no signs of wear.

6. Tulip, made by Tennie Jane Fuller, ca. 1870s.
   Total size: 70″ by 90″.
   The family name for this quilt is "Diamond Tulip." It is pieced of red and green cottons on a white background. There are twelve blocks in the piece, three across and four down. This quilt is in excellent condition, even though the green has faded somewhat to a greenish-tan. The sashes and borders are composed of red and green strips in the order: red-green-red. The corner blocks of each sash are small nine-patch red and green blocks. The

quilting is very fine and the quilt is closely quilted in an almost stippled effect. The binding is hand sewn of the greenish-tan cotton.

7. Mexican Rose, made by Tennie Jane Fuller, ca. 1870s.[11]
Total size: 75″ by 83″.
This lovely old quilt is one of three applique quilts in the group and is, by far, the oldest. The family name for this quilt is "Daisy" and it is made of red, yellow, white and brown cottons. The brown may have been green originally. There are six full and three half rose groups. Family history places the quilt in the late 1870s or very early 1880s. The border treatment is the same as on the Tulip also made by Tennie Jane. Each rose consists of four six-petaled red flowers. The flowers have yellow centers on stems which are now brown. The stems each bear two small brown leaves and meets on the diagonal in the yellow center. Four large brown leaves emerge from the center and point to the four points of the compass. The background and backing fabric is white cotton. The quilting is very fine. It follows the design and fills the white background areas with outline and cross-hatch. The quilt is in excellent condition. The set of the borders is unusual, as are the half roses along one side.

8. Anna's Irish Tulip, made by Mattie Fuller Andrews, ca. 1930s.
Total size: 70″ by 80″.
The family name for this quilt is Dutch Tulip. It is hand pieced of a sea green and three shades of pink cotton solids. There are fifteen tulip blocks in six rows. They alternate with solid green blocks in a pattern of three tulips-two solids on one row, then, two tulips-three solids on the next. The background for the tulip blocks is pale pink. The stems and leaves are green with the tulip flower being composed of a medium and dark pink. There is a double row of outline quilting around the flowers and along the inner block edges. The rest of the quilt is done in cross-hatch quilting set 1⅛ inches apart. The quilt is sun faded along the right side. Mrs. Palmer said it was used as a bedspread in a room with western exposure. The quilting is very good and the fabric is in good condition, despite the sun faded areas.

9. Dutch Doll, made by Mattie Fuller Andrews, ca. late 1920s.
Total size: 64″ by 80″.
This quilt is made of pieces of Mrs. Palmer's first grade dresses

and was made for her by her grandmother. It is now in the possession of her daughter. There are thirty dolls set in five rows of six each. The dolls are appliqued to lavendar blocks. The backing fabric is also lavender. The figures are outlined in a black buttonhole stitch and the background is done in a fine crosshatch. This quilt shows signs of wear.

10. Double Wedding Ring, made by Mattie Fuller Andrews, ca. 1932.
Total size: 76" by 92".
This quilt is machine pieced of 1930s cotton prints and solids. The hand quilting is done in outline stitching around the rings and in curved lines within the rings. The background fabric is a vibrant green. There are twenty rings. The binding is machine sewn of the same fabric as the background and backing fabrics. This quilt is in excellent condition with no signs of use or wear.

11. Goose Tracks, made by Abbie Fuller Blanton, ca. 1920.
Total size: 70" by 80".
This hand pieced and quilted creation is the only one in the group in which an intentional mistake can be detected in the piecing. One corner has one of the tracks turned upside down. There are twenty blocks of pink and green solid "tracks" set in white. The borders are composed of pink-white-green strips with pink corner squares. The quilting is done in an outline pattern. This quilt, too, is in near perfect condition.

12. Texas Tears, made by Abbie Fuller Blanton, ca. 1920s.
Total size: 67" by 80".
Hand pieced and quilted in an outline pattern this quilt is composed of pink solids and a pink and white rosebud print. The backing is the same rosebud print. The condition of the quilt is very good. This pattern is also known as Job's Tears.[12]

13. Friendship Quilt, made in April 1912.
Total size: 70" by 82".
This quilt is the only one in the collection made for one of the ladies instead of by one of them. It was made in Weatherford, Texas, a small town west of Fort Worth, in April 1912 by the family of Rev. Hugh Bryant Prather as a wedding gift for the minister and his new wife, Vada Andrews Prather.[13] This quilt is in excellent condition because, according to Mrs. Palmer, it was stored by her mother and never used. The fabrics are red cot-

ton, muslin and a variety of prints. The pattern is an embroidered album patch. Names are embroidered on the muslin centers of each block. The sashes are red with muslin corner blocks. There are a total of twenty signed blocks in the piece.

14. Dresden Plate, made by Vada Andrews Prather, ca. 1935.
    Total size: 66″ by 82″.
    This quilt is hand pieced of assorted 1930s dress prints on a green background. The hand quilting around the twenty plates is predominately outline quilting, with some simple decorative quilting done between the plates. There is evidence of some fabric deterioration on two plates due to sun exposure. The quilt is in generally good condition despite the fading along one side.

15. Fruit Basket, made by Vada Andrews Prather, ca. late 1920s– early 1930s.
    Total size: 72″ by 82″.
    This quilt was made from a pattern ordered from a ladies magazine in the late 1920s, and was possibly a kit quilt. There are 28 baskets containing thirteen types of appliqued fruit, decorated with embroidery. The fruits depicted are: apples, peaches, lemons, oranges, cherries, bananas, pineapples, grapes, strawberries, limes, figs, quinces, and three colors of plums. The background fabrics are tan and dark brown cotton. The baskets are made of a medium brown cotton and done in block form, set on point. Quilting designs consist of outline and cross-hatch. The fabrics of this quilt are in good condition, though one side is slightly sun faded.

16. Grandmother's Flower Garden, made by Vada Andrews Prather, ca. 1938.
    Total size: 76″ by 85″.
    This lovely quilt is composed of multicolored cotton print flowers set in a white background. Each hexagon in the flowers is ¾ inch across. The borders are composed of three shades of lavender with the darkest shade also used for the quilt back. The sides and botton of the quilt are finished in a zig-zag motif. Mrs. Palmer says this was the last quilt her mother made and was intended for use as a bedspread. However, it was never used.

Notes and References:

1. The Dallas Morning News, *The Texas Almanac, 1984–1985*; (Dallas, A.H. Belo Corp. 1984), pp. 71, 160–161, 186, 236, 171.
2. Conversation with Mrs. Hilda Palmer, April 1984.
3. Conversation with Mr. Oliver McReynolds, July 1984.
4. Ibid.
5. Debbie Lynn Fields, *Neches City Cemetery*, unpublished paper from Palestine, Texas, Public Library, p. 22.
6. Conversation with Mrs. Hilda Palmer, March 1984.
7. *Ibid.*
8. *Ibid.*
9. *Ibid.*
10. Conversation with Mrs. Hilda Palmer, April 1984.
11. Yvonne M. Khin, *Collector's Dictionary of Quilt Names and Patterns* (Washington, Acropolis Books, 1980), p. 329.
12. Beverly Ann Orbelo, *A Texas Quilting Primer* (San Antonio, Corona Publishing Company, 1982), p. 21.
13. Conversation with Mrs. Hilda Palmer, March 1984.

18th Century Quilted Silk Petticoats Worn in America

Tandy Hersh

Averil Colby's book *Quilting* documents the history of quilted wearing apparel from a possible 3400 B.C. date in Egypt to the 20th century. Quilted garments have been used for padding to help deflect ancient weapons, as a cushion under armor to make the armor wearer more comfortable, and the several layers stitched together have formed an insulation against the cold.[1] Quilted petticoats had been a part of this clothing history as warm undergarments when a new decorative external use was made of them in the high styles of the 18th century. After this brief flourishing of the petticoat as a fashionable outer garment, it continued as a warm undergarment into the 20th century.

This paper's focus is on decorative exposed quilted silk petticoats worn in America in the period of exaggerated fashion styles for both men and women. The puritan ban on any ornamenting of clothing with lace, metal thread, cut work, embroidery, or any revealing of the body,[2] no longer applied, and excesses of low neck lines, tightly corseted bodices and unnatural contours through use of hoops were in vogue. With some hoops extending four feet on each side, cartoonists of the day noted the extreme size.[3] Elegant silks were featured in waistcoats for men, and in ensembles for women. American colonists emulated the fashions of England and the continent, using clothes to indicate power and social status.[4]

The quilted silk petticoat was not designed to be a practical garment, so instead of being worn threadbare and destroyed, some were carefully put away, and eventually given to a historical society, a museum, or entered a private collection, consequently being pre-

Martha Tandy Hersh: 1860 Walnut Bottom Rd, Carlisle, PA 17013

served for study. The Boston Museum of Fine Arts, Colonial Williamsburg Foundation, DAR Museum, Los Angeles County Museum of Art, Smithsonian Institution, and historical societies in West Chester and Philadelphia, Pennsylvania, Hartford, Connecticut, and Newport and Providence, Rhode Island are a few of the many places where the petticoats can be seen.

Naively, perhaps, at the outset of this research, one aim was to discover the country of origin for each petticoat and to examine it for characteristics peculiar to England, France, Italy, or America, for example. However, museum documents did not provide adequate information on the quilters or their countries. The research shifted to a search for other evidence of origins: physical characteristics, construction types, quilting designs, and examination of outstanding examples.

Because the American colonies were under British rule the entire period of the exposed petticoat style, it seemed reasonable to study the design sources, needlework techniques, embroidery patterns, and quilted articles that were used in England in the 17th and 18th centuries that could have been brought to America and in turn used to influence quilters here. This approach will be followed here. We should recognize the contributions of other countries to England and America, but it was impossible within present constraints to study the development of silk cloth, examine fashion prints, or trace the movement of competent sewing craftspeople who carried fashion ideas from one country to another.

One interesting example of a method of exchanging new styles was through the use of fashion miniatures on dolls. A doll was dressed in France, for instance, in a current adult style, and sent to another country to show what was being worn in France. Marie Antoinette sent one to her mother and sisters in Austria. England exported some dolls to the Czarina in Russia, and one was advertised in a 1733 issue of *The New England Journal* in Boston. It had arrived by ship from London and could be seen, by paying a fee, at the mantua maker's shop.[5] Colonial Williamsburg has a doll with a linen chemise, a set of pockets, an under petticoat, the exposed quilted petticoat, dress, hat and shoes.[6] From these miniatures, a customer could have her seamstress copy the style.

The height of popularity for the decorative quilted petticoat in England was mid-18th century, with a few being worn before 1710 or after 1775.[7] Establishing a comparable period in America is difficult. An early fragment associated with John and Priscilla Alden's daughter is dated "ca 1685–1720."[8] Other museum examples have indefinite dates also and some simply say "18th century." However, inventories suggest a period roughly parallel with England. There is an impressive study of 10,788 inventories of the 11,313 estates of Chester County, Pennsylvania which were filed in West Chester and Philadelphia, Pennsylvania, between 1684 and 1849. From 1700 to 1800 there are 4,627 inventories and only 28 entries of quilted petticoats: 10 in the 1740s, 7 in the 1750s, 3 in the 1760s, 5 in the 1770s, and 3 Marseilles petticoats, 1 in the 1780s, and 2 in the 1790s. Only two identify the material, one silk and one "linsey." The rest are entered as quilted, or by color, followed by the word quilted. Some of these could be utilitarian rather than ornamental.[9] In Cumberland County, Pennsylvania, only eight entries for quilted petticoats were found in 450 18th century inventories studied.

Inventories in the 1700s noted household textiles and clothing found in the deceased's estate because of the relatively high value placed on these items at that time. Those in Cumberland County often described the item's condition as "new," "half worn," "worn," and "old," showing that worn or old textiles still had value. Since so few quilted petticoats, ornamental or utilitarian, are listed, in any condition, it suggests that they were rather rare in this period.

From the above observations we can conclude that in America as in Europe, quilted silk petticoats were included in high style ornamental clothing, that quilted petticoats from this period remain in museums, and there is useful evidence in inventories in the mid-1700s. In addition a search of the published literature indicates that this particular garment has not been studied widely in America.

Physical Characteristics

The top surface of a typical 18th century ornamental petticoat was made of solid color plain or satin weave silk. Carded wool fibers were used for filling and the lining was most often solid color glazed or unglazed wool material. A rectangle approximately 33 inches by 100 inches was quilted with matching color silk thread. A narrow piece of unquilted silk with wool lining, but no filling, was stitched to the long side of the quilted base. Before this unquilted material was pleated and sewn to a waist band, two eight inch side openings were made, either at seam lines or cut into the quilting. These pocket slits and the hem were bound with matching color silk ribbon. Tapes were sewn on both sides of these openings to tie the garment at the waist. The openings permitted the wearer to reach through the petticoat to a pair of large pockets which were attached to a long tape and tied at the waist underneath the petticoat. Many of the petticoats studied have replacement hem bindings, waist bands and ties because of wear or being altered for taller and shorter ladies. The construction steps are illustrated in *Costume in Detail, Women's Dress 1730–1930.*[10]

The petticoat became an exposed garment when the dress skirt front was separated to form an inverted V or wedge shape panel from the waist to the hem. More of the petticoat showed at the bottom edge. As different style hoops became fashionable, varying amounts of the petticoat showed, but it was in the lower third, or border, that the designing and quilting expertise was concentrated. The remaining two thirds were filled with a simple repeated pattern of diamonds, squares set on point, shells, or curving lines.

The proportion of border to overall design area reflects earlier non-quilted petticoat design. There are references to one petticoat in England having nine rows of fringe at the lower edge, and in France examples with single and multiple lace flounces in the border.[11] Another petticoat had "three borders to the tail."[12] In some cases embroidered bands were sewn to the lower edge. A deep flounce was placed at the hem on another.[13] All of these decorative additions accented horizontal lines. The 1695 English Kimberly petticoat, which is not quilted, used a horizontal weft striped wool fabric with every other narrow stripe embroidered with silver-gilt thread from the hem to the knee area forming a border. The matching gown made of the same fabric, though unembroidered, was cut so the stripes were in the vertical position, contrasting with the horizontal ones in the petticoat. French prints illustrating the Kimberly dress article show fringes and flounces in other gown-petticoat combinations, emphasizing the design feature at the floor.[14] Most of the 18th century quilted petticoats studied continued using this proportion by making the border design more dominant than the upper two thirds.

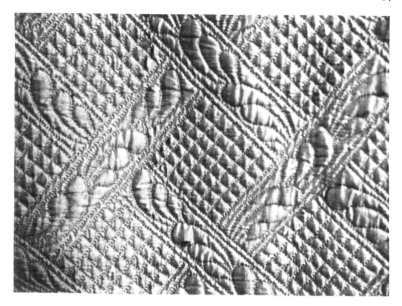

Fig. 1. Detail, gold silk petticoat fragment, #3622 in the collections of the DAR Museum, showing repeat pattern above the border design. Donor: Mrs. Robert M. Weber.

Types

At least five different types of quilted petticoat were worn in the 18th century. Four of these were hand stitched and one was machine woven. I will discuss them in this sequence: running stitch, stuffed work, cord quilting, machine woven or Marseilles, and a variant type which employs several different stitches.

Running stitch petticoats are those on which the only quilting stitch used was the running stitch. They are the most numerous and are found in collections in England and America. Museum accession cards assign probable origin as "English," "Possibly English," "American," and "Possibly American." Family history gives documentation of where and when a petticoat was worn, but it does not locate where it was made. Since there are records of quilted petticoats being imported from England,[15] the fabrics used for lining and the skill in drawing designs and in quilting must be examined to help establish the probable origins of the first three types listed.

Stuffed work petticoats were quilted with running stitch and are also found in England and America. Cotton or wool fibers were carefully stuffed, from the lining side, into parts of previously outlined designs, creating high and low relief in the border. The overall repeated design was not stuffed.

Cord-quilted petticoats, like the two previous types, were quilted with running stitch and are found in England and America. The distinguishing feature of this group was made by first quilting close parallel rows of running stitches in a desired pattern in the border and then threading a small cord through the channel between the two running stitch rows. This made elevated ridges in the border, contrasting with the running stitch overall repeated top pattern. The stuffed work and cord-quilted petticoats studied used running stitch. However other petticoats in these two types could have been made with back stitch.[16]

The fourth type is *silk double-cloth yardage*, simulating hand quilting, but woven on looms in England and France.[17] These petticoats observed the same proportion of the small repeated pattern in the top two thirds, and the elaborate border in the bottom one third. The fabric was woven with the ornamental border pattern threaded on one side of the warp and the repeated pattern extending to the opposite selvedge. The top silk warp was densely set and the bottom silk warp had fewer threads per inch. As these two warps interacted, a third yarn, corresponding to the filling of the three layered hand quilted product, was woven in. This yarn was a soft unplied cotton. A proper length for the width of a petticoat was cut off the woven yardage, turned, so a selvedge and the border were at the bottom edge, and then the same construction details were followed as for the hand sewn product.

I have termed the fifth type *variant*, because only variations of the back stitch were used in the border. This was the most time consuming of the stitching techniques because every back stitch was made as a separate stitch. The overall pattern in the top of these petticoats was made with running stitch, the one common quilting feature of the four handmade types. All of the stitches on the front surface of a variant type petticoat appear to be running stitches, that is, the thread surfaces for one stitch, then disappears to the back for one stitch and reappears on the surface for one stitch. Close examination of the border, however, shows that each surface stitch is a tiny individual back stitch, surrounded by plain fabric. This means that on each stitch all of the thread had to be pulled through the fabric before moving to the next stitch.

Turning to the lining side, running stitches show in the repeated pattern area, but only variations of the reverse side of back stitch are in the border area. There are rows of parallel slanting stitches, both left to right and right to left, rows of parallel horizontal stitches, and rows of solid quilting thread with no fabric showing between the stitches. All of the variant petticoats studied have closely spaced diagonal rows of background quilting in the border which make the designs stand out. As the lining side of a petticoat was not to be seen the way the underside of a quilt was seen, knots, ends of threads and long threads connecting two rows are visible. The variant type was made in wool as well as in silk.

There must have been a reason for quilting in an exacting method which took more time and used more thread. Perhaps the detail found in the complicated designs on the variant petticoats could not have been executed without stitch by stitch control in the outlining. A second reason could be the desire to compact the layers more to give a firmer texture than running stitch does. On one variant petticoat there are 16–18 surface back stitches per inch in the border, and 10–11 surface running stitches in the overall repeated top pattern area, with four lines of diagonal ground quilting in one half inch in the border.

During the Irene Emery Round Table on Museum Textiles held in the Textile Museum in Washington, D.C. in 1975, three petticoats from the DAR Museum were contrasted: one stuffed work, one running stitch and one variant stitch. Anne Pollard Rowe wrote a monograph, "American Quilted Petticoats," reporting on the discussion. She referred to the stuffed work and running stitch example as "English type" and the variant examples as "American type," without mentioning the stitch construction. One of the reasons for this English-American designation was that Natalie Rothstein of the Victoria and Albert Museum and Cora Ginsberg, an American textile authority, said that they were not aware of any petticoats of the "American type" in English collections.[18] The variant petticoats in this paper's study were found only in Massachusetts, Connecticut, Rhode Island, and New Jersey.

A variety of quilting effects resulted from the five types examined. The running stitch produced uniform relief. Stuffed work and cord

Fig. 2. Yellow silk petticoat, accession #52–19 in collections of the Colonial Williamsburg Foundation. "Abigail Trowbridge 1750" quilted in a border. Photo courtesy Colonial Williamsburg Foundation.

quilting added elements that gave different shaped contours. Woven petticoats duplicated the relief of the running stitch but with perfect uniformity. The variant type expanded the design possibilities by achieving more detail. Stuffed work, cord quilting, and the variant type added firmness to the garment.

Designs

The inspiration for the designs probably came from books, earlier textiles, and metal work. Plates from scientific horticulture, animal, and bird books from Europe and England, embroidered motifs on 16th and 17th century English clothing articles and designs on metal items, such as a 17th century silver stand in the Boston Museum of

Fine Arts,[19] were available for interpretation in quilting. An illumination, "The Parliament of Beasts" circa 1480, and a hand colored woodcut of birds, circa 1485, show unicorns, stags with antlers, boars, horses, a snake, a dog, a rabbit, a lion, peacocks, roosters, storks, griffins, ducks, swans, an eagle, etc.[20] Patterns were made for a wide variety of natural and mythical animal forms found on similar sources and were traced on fabric for embroidery work. A late 16th century English embroidered coif (head covering), has six large fruit, flower and berry trees, with a lion, a lioness, snails, a monkey, a bird with a worm in its beak, grasshoppers, squirrels, snakes, rabbits, moths, and birds sitting on perches arranged as spot motifs with no regard for scale. A bunch of grapes is larger than a lion and the berry tree has a large lily blossom the same size as the berry.[21] On early 17th century English ladies' jackets embroidered vines form a pattern of cyma curves. Flowers placed in the curves appear to be framed by the vines. Birds and animals perch on the vines and insects fly around them.[22]

Fruit, flowers, leaves, feathers, and curving vines were used as the fundamental designs which were quilted on the running stitch, stuffed work, and cord quilted petticoats studied. These designs were also quilted on the variant petticoats, but, in addition, the variant group featured exotic designs. Dragons, unicorns, snakes, confronting animals, sailing ships, mermaids, heraldry motifs, peacocks, with added touches such as three tiny circles on a snake's head, and a lady in a quilted petticoat record the imagination and skill of the variant petticoat designers and quilters. As in the embroidery examples the scale was not realistic and the designs were most often randomly placed.

Some animals are quilted with skeletal rib cages which help distinguish this group from others. Mildred B. Lanier used an illustration of a wool quilted petticoat that has two of the skeletal bodied animals surrounded by closely spaced diagonal ground rows and classified the garment as an example of first generation Marseilles, (a hand quilted textile that influenced Marseilles woven pattern designing).[23] Her reference, Anne Rowe's reference to country of origin, American type, and this paper's discussion of the variant stitch are all descriptions of the same type textile.

Examples

There are many examples of quilted petticoats in public collections. The Chester County Historical Society in West Chester,
Pennsylvania, owns Ann Marsh's pale blue silk running stitch petticoat.[24] She was born in England in 1717, and died in 1797 in Chester
County. Her petticoat is lined with a deep blue wool material. There
are four pieces of a 30-inch-wide silk sewn together to make a lower
edge of 120 inches. Two 23 inch tall patterns (more than the usual
border width) were quilted and repeated one time and 10 inches of
overall squares set on point was added as a pattern for the top. The
design was centered on the seam and the 15 inches on each side
were filled with pomegranates, sunflowers, tulips, leaves, and vines
growing out of two different urns. Close diagonal lines were quilted
for a ground to make the design stand out, and the direction of
these lines changed at the seam.

The Costume Division of the Smithsonian has a very similar
running stitch petticoat with Virginia provenance, also in pale blue
silk with darker blue wool lining. It is ornamented similarly with
two urns and an enlarged design of sunflowers.[25] Both petticoats
have a scalloped design at the hem. The Virginia petticoat designs
are not centered on the seam, but it is possible these petticoats were
made from the same distinctive pattern, if not made by the same
person. A more careful comparison needs to be made.

Chester County Historical Society has a beige quilted silk doll
petticoat made from an adult's petticoat.[26] It is 8¾ inches long, has a
6 inch waist and is 20 inches around the hem. Its backing is apricot
wool. It is running stitch and the date 1825 is pinned to it. At least
one family was willing to cut up an out-of-fashion garment for a
child's pleasure.

Another recycling of the out of date fashion is also at Chester
County. It is a bed covering made by cutting a running stitch petticoat in half, and sewing the two hem edges together, then framing
the resultant rectangle with an appropriate material.[27] There are
other examples of this use at Winterthur Museum, Winterthur,
Delaware, and the John Brown house, Providence, Rhode Island.

The DAR Museum has a variant petticoat fragment 57 by 29½
inches, perhaps half or three-fifths of the original width.[28] This gold
quilted silk rectangle has three 19 inch wide designs along the lower

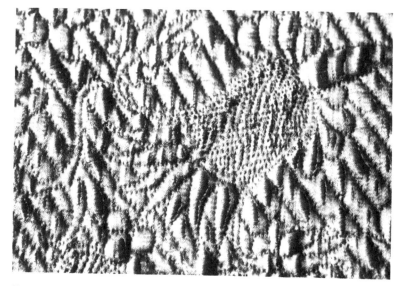

Fig. 3. Detail, dark blue silk petticoat fragment in collections of the Newport Historical Society, Rhode Island.

Fig. 4. Detail, reverse side of Figure 3, showing example of the variant stitch.

edge. The first 19 inches contains a three-masted sailing ship on a wave filled ocean, with a bare breasted mermaid holding a comb. The comb has 12 rows of teeth in 5/8th of an inch. A school of fish or porpoises and a bird sitting on the water are near the ship. There are five birds flying over the ship; one has a fish in its mouth, another one is diving. A banner flies from a tall mast, and an ensign from the stern. The second 19 inch panel has a tree with four large pineapple-like forms growing with unreal flowers and leaves. Below the tree are a lion, a rabbit, and a bird. The third 19 inch panel has a pear tree with 14 large pears and a unicorn and a greyhound below it. A cusped band separates the border from the overall pattern. The overall pattern on this fragment is laid out in large squares set on point, subdivided into 49 small squares, with a plume or feather design surrounding each large square, making a most elaborate upper grid. (Fig. 1) It is an exquisite piece of quilting and designing. A detail of the ship panel and a quilting pattern for the ship only are in the *Woman's Day Book of American Needlework* and in the accompanying box of patterns.[29]

The Victoria and Albert Museum has a 1703 English back and running stitch linen quilt with embroidered silk designs. Around the border in architectural arches are 16 quilted designs. A three-masted sailing vessel, a mermaid with mirror, and a panel of fish are in three of the arches.[30] Though the DAR petticoat and the quilt share designs, the back of the petticoat suggests that it was not made in England, at least not for export. The lining was made of two different blue and cream striped wool fabrics, one cut into many pieces, two dark blue wool scraps and a small piece of checked linen near the waist band.

Another example of the variant category is at Colonial Williamsburg. (Fig. 2) It is pale yellow silk lined with yellow wool, and its unique feature is the quilting of the name "Abigail Trowbridge 1750" in a cusped band between the border and the overall top squares set on point pattern. The words "Honi soit qui mal y pens[e]" are quilted around a crowned circle, with a confronting lion and unicorn on either side. This is an adaptation of the royal arms of England. In another place on the border a man in a waistcoat and knee breeches is doffing his tricorn hat to a lady in a quilted petticoat. Animals are quilted at intervals near the hem binding.[31]

The Newport Rhode Island Historical Society has a small frag-

Fig. 5. Motifs from border of petticoat, accession #323525 in collections of the Smithsonian Institution. Author's drawing.

ment of dark blue silk, lined with dark blue wool quilted in variant stitch. (Figures 3 and 4) The work on this piece rivals any for both art and needlework. The designs are only flowers, vines, and leaves. Perhaps the fragment is so small that no animals remain, or it was made without the animal designs. Family history associates this petticoat with Anstes Ellery who was born in 1697 and married John Almy in 1716.[32]

The petticoat with the most designs, is a gold silk variant type worn in Connecticut around 1730. It is in the Textile Division of the Smithsonian Institution.[33] There is no small repeated design on it at all, only fanciful designs surrounded by diagonal lines of ground quilting. All 33 by 98 inches are quilted with dragons, squirrels, lions, roosters, insects, rabbits, peacocks, dogs, frogs, horses, unicorns, cows, flying and standing birds, butterflies, snakes, boars, antlered stags, a bird pecking its breast, carnations, tulips, grapes, strawberries, vines, pomegranates and plumes. The designs are out-

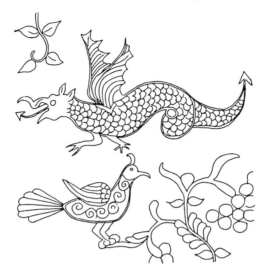

Fig. 6. Motifs from border of petticoat, accession #323525 in collections of the Smithsonian Institution. Author's drawing.

lined with close double rows of variant stitches and the detail is exceptional. There are finely drawn manes, spines on the boars' backs, shell quilting in some animal bodies, and the characteristic skeletal rib cages between fully fleshed out back and front legs of many animals found in the variant group. (Figures 5 and 6) The dragon's tongue and tail end in an arrow design seen in English art forms during the Tudor era.[34]

The variant type petticoat merits continuing study. Of the twelve examples that are known to me, only six have been studied from the lining side. A systematic analysis of all of these, plus correspondence with the many small museums in New England in an effort to locate others, will be a beginning. A diary with an entry about working on a petticoat, or having received a finished petticoat, or a statement about paying for materials could be in the holdings of a historical society along with the actual petticoat. An effort to understand "French Quiltings," a technique taught in Boston in 1771 when Anna Green Winslow wrote her diary,[35] a search for genealogical material on "Abigail Trowbridge 1750" and an examination of the petticoat in Mildred B. Lanier's article will be made. A thorough study of the stitching technique on all the variant type group of petticoats may lead to an answer as to whether this work was done by skilled needlewomen for themselves or by professional designers and quilters.

Notes and References:

1. Averil Colby, *Quilting* (London: Batsford, 1972), pp. 1–19.
2. Alice Morse Earle, *Customs and Fashions in Old New England* (New York: Charles Scribner's Sons, 1894), p. 316.
3. Edward Warwick, Henry C. Pitz, Alexander Wyckoff, *Early American Dress* (New York: Benjamin Blom, 1965), plates 61A and B, 64A and B.
4. Edward Maeder, *An Elegant Art: Fashion and Fantasy in the Eighteenth Century* (New York: Los Angeles County Museum of Art in association with Harry N. Abrams, Inc., 1983), p. 15.
5. Dorothy Smith Coleman, "Fashion Dolls/Fashionable Dolls," *Dress*, Vol. 3/1977, pp. 1–8.
6. Document Textile C66–386, Colonial Williamsburg Foundation.
7. C. Willett and Phillis Cunnington, *Handbook of English Costume in 18th Century* (London: Faber and Faber, Ltd., 1964), pp. 116, 138.
8. Museum of Fine Arts, *New England Begins: The Seventeenth Century* (Boston: Museum of Fine Arts, 1982), Vol. 2, p. 348.
9. Margaret B. Schiffer, *Chester County, Pennsylvania Inventories 1684–1850* (Exton, Pa.: Schiffer Publishing, Ltd., 1974), p. 36, pp. 66–67.
10. Nancy Bradfield, *Costume in Detail, Women's Dress 1730–1930* (Boston: Barnes and Noble, Inc., 1971), pp. 21–26.
11. Adolph S. Cavallo, "The Kimberly Gown," *Metropolitan Museum Journal*, 3-1970, p. 214.
12. Ann Buck, *Dress in 18th Century England* (New York: Holmes and Meier, 1979), p. 133.
13. Cunnington, p. 112.

14. Cavallo, pp. 199–217.
15. Ann Pollard Rowe, "American Quilted Petticoats," Irene Emery Roundtable on Museum Textiles 1975 *Proceedings* LC76–56646, p. 162.
16. Susan Burrows Swan, *Plain and Fancy* (New York: Holt, Rinehart and Winston, 1977), pp. 224, 233.
17. Sally Garoutte, "Marseilles Quilts and their Woven Offspring," *Uncoverings 1982* (Mill Valley, Ca.: American Quilt Study Group, 1983), pp. 115–134.
18. Rowe, pp. 161–65.
19. Museum of Fine Arts, Boston, *New England Begins: The Seventeenth Century* (Boston: Museum of Fine Arts, 1982), Vol. 3, pp. 499–500.
20. Francis Donald Klingender, *Animals in Art and Thought to the End of the Middle Ages* (London: Routledge and Kegan Paul, 1971), pp. 211, 304.
21. Document Textile D331, Victoria and Albert Museum, London.
22. Document Textile 1359-1900, Victoria and Albert Museum, London.
23. Mildred B. Lanier, "Marseilles Quiltings of the 18th and 19th Century" *Bulletin de Liaison du CIETA*, #47/48, 1978, p. 75.
24. Document Textile P52, Chester County Historical Society, West Chester,. Pa.
25. Document Textile 251939.2, Smithsonian Institution.
26. Document Textile, Chester County Historical Society, West Chester, Pa.
27. Document Textile A200/69, Chester County Historical Society, West Chester, Pa.
28. Document Textile 3622, DAR Museum.
29. Rose Wilder Lane, *Woman's Day Book of American Needlework* (New York: Simon and Schuster, 1963), p. 117.
30. Document Textile 1564-1902, Victoria and Albert Museum, London.
31. Document Textile 52-19, Colonial Williamsburg Foundation.
32. Document Textile, Newport Historical Society, Newport, Rhode Island.
33. Document Textile 323525, Smithsonian Institution.
34. Encyclopedia Britannica (Chicago: William Benton, 1963), Vol. 11, p. 469.
35. Alice Morse Earle, ed. *Diary of a Boston School Girl* (Boston: Houghton Mifflin and Co., 1894), p. 105.

Characteristics of Missouri-German Quilts
Suellen Meyer

The Missouri River winds eastward through the heart of Missouri cutting the state in half north and south. When the first American settlers from Kentucky arrived in the early 1800s, they chose the land north of the river which reminded them of home; Tennesseeans settled farther south in the Ozarks and the Bootheel of Missouri. The land bordering the river was settled sparsely by frontiers-people, those hardy ones who would stay for a few years, hack out a farm, and then move when anyone got too close. Thus, when the Germans arrived seeking their fortunes in the 1830s, the river land was waiting for them.

Many German-American descendants still live where their ancestors settled on the Missouri river, in villages and towns with names that reminded them of home: Rhineland, Dutzow, Berger, Holstein, Hermann. Most of the smaller towns are dying while the larger ones, like Hermann, are suffering from fast-food franchises and uncontrolled subdivisions. The German culture, though respected, is becoming a thing apart, celebrated in festivals, reminisced over, but no longer an everyday part of life.

Until World War I, the area was thoroughly German in culture. Everyone spoke German. School lessons and church services were conducted in German. When America entered the war, however, the Missouri-Germans chose to speak English to demonstrate their loyalty. Now, people in their seventies and eighties are fluent in German and English; their children may speak and understand German but not be able to read it; their grandchildren know only English.

For some years I had wondered about the quilts made by the Missouri-German women. How did the Germans learn to quilt?

Suellen Meyer: 11210 Still Lane, Creve Coeur, MO 63141

How important were quilts to their lives? What did the quilts look like? In 1982, I had the chance to find the answers to my questions. Funded by a grant from the American Association of University Women, I visited with women in the small towns on the river from St. Charles to Jefferson City, photographed their quilts, and asked them about their lives. (Figure 1)

Historical Background

The great wave of German immigration lasted from the 1830s through the 1850s. Thousands came directly from western Germany and Switzerland to settle along the Missouri River valley. They left Germany to escape its political and economic upheavals; they came to Missouri largely because Gottfried Duden told them to. When Duden, a well-to-do lawyer from the district of Mulheim, decided that the German common people needed to leave Germany to improve their lot, he set himself the task of choosing a likely spot for them to settle. In 1824, he followed the American migration westward from Baltimore to St. Louis where he was favorably impressed with the land. Soon he bought a farm in Montgomery County (now Warren County) where he lived for two years. Since he was wealthy, he hired people to do the onerous tasks like clearing land and planting, leaving him free to travel, to meet Americans, and to study the area. When he returned to Germany, he wrote one of the generation's most influential books, *Report on a Journey to the Western States of North America*, in which he extolled the abundance of Missouri, its fertile land, and its friendly Anglo-American settlers. Thousands of his German followers came to Missouri in the next twenty years, most going directly to land on the Missouri River where they bought farms from the first movement of Anglo-American pioneers who were ready to move farther west.

Before the Anglos moved on, they taught the Germans techniques for taming the Missouri land—ways of felling trees, building fences, rolling logs, and stacking corn shocks, skills that the cultivated land in Germany no longer required.[1] If the men worked this closely together, it is likely that the women also met to share domestic knowledge; most likely this is how German women who had no tradition of quiltmaking learned to piece and to quilt.

We tend to think of the Germans as a homogeneous group en-

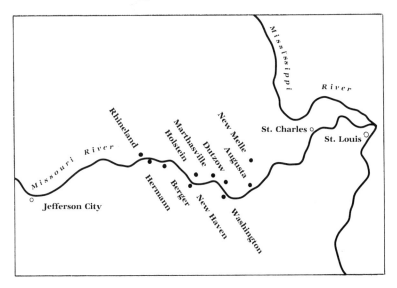

Fig. 1. German towns on the Lower Missouri River included in this study.

tirely separate from the Americans. This is not true. Several nine-teenth-century writers speak of the friendly relations between the two groups.[2] Nor is it true that the Germans themselves were homo-geneous. Some were aristocrats, others artisans, and still others peasants. Some spoke High German and others Low German. (The languages sometimes caused problems. When Mrs. Clara Kuschel began teaching in New Haven, she had to learn to speak Low German so she could communicate with the children in the town; later when she married, she and her husband spoke Low German to the family and High German when they didn't want the children to understand.[3] Because they had come from such diverse German provinces as Hanover, Prussia, Westphalia, Bavaria, and Saxony, their customs, attitudes, and beliefs were often quite different.[4]

When the German women began making quilts, their quilts were more like those of their American neighbors than unlike them; the variety of German traditions probably diluted the impact of any one design tradition.

Over time the newcomers kept some social customs from Germany, while adapting American farming and cooking methods to their needs, and learning to make quilts. In Germany, people kept warm under woven coverlets, not quilts. In Missouri, both American and German women were notable weavers who wove not only coverlets but also heavy linen or cotton sheets and light woolen blankets.[5] In fact, home weaving was so common that weavers were warned not to immigrate to Missouri seeking work.[6]

For a time, women used both quilts and coverlets. Elsa Scheer of New Haven told me her mother gave each daughter feather pillows, coverlets, and three quilts when she married and that she had used all of hers.[7] Although everyone agrees that coverlets were brought from Germany, the origin of quiltmaking within the German community is not clear. At least one nineteenth-century writer refers to quilting bees in the German community, but he does so only in passing.[8]

None of the women I interviewed had an explanation for the making of the first Missouri-German quilts, but they were definite about how they learned to make quilts; their mothers taught them. They began by learning to piece. The winter she was eight, Gertrude Allgeyer and her sister pieced Four-Patch blocks which their mother later set together and quilted for them. They made so many blocks that each got two full-sized quilts.[9] Women recognized quiltmaking as an important skill. Even when a woman did not have time to quilt herself, she taught her daughters. Mrs. Herbert Kloppe of New Haven recalled, "I showed all my girls how to quilt, but with ten children I didn't have time to quilt myself."[10]

Beginnings of Missouri-German Quiltmaking

Very few nineteenth-century quilts have survived. In fact, of the 214 quilts I recorded, only twenty were made before 1900 and of these, only six before 1880. These dates are, of course, approximate. They come from family stories and from examining the textiles used in making the quilts.

The nineteenth-century quilts that have survived do not appear significantly different in design from the twentieth-century quilts. Only two (10 percent) of the twenty are appliqued; seven (35 percent) are stars. (In twentieth-century quilts, 7 percent are appliqued and 20 percent are stars.) One is clearly a masterpiece quilt which has been carefully preserved. Agnes Struckhoff says it is her grandmother's bridal quilt made in 1858.[10] A North Carolina Lily, it has an appliqued border of flowers, vines, and birds. It is unusual in the Missouri-German area both for its elaborate design and for its age.

Other quilts may have survived because they were made for a special occasion—although that reason has been lost. Or it's possible that they survived through mere chance. I saw a collection of late nineteenth-century and early twentieth-century quilts at a farmhouse in Franklin County. When Regina Bolton Sullentrop died, her son stopped using her quilts, putting them away in bureau drawers where they remained until his death in 1984. These quilts, already worn from everyday use, would not have survived much more wear.

Actually, it may be surprising that any nineteenth-century quilts exist. Duden's first winter here (1824–25) was exceptionally mild; some immigrants, reading his account, believed such winters were the rule rather than the exception and arrived with few winter bedclothes. According to one respondent, they spent the winter struggling to keep warm and cursing Duden's advice.[12] If true, this story suggests that the climate demanded women make immediate provision for warm covers. But the climate was not the only demanding element of the new environment; the land was all-absorbing. Because Duden had not done his own work but had hired it, he grossly underestimated the sheer physical labor that creating a farm from virgin forest required. As women were active partners in the farms, they too spent hours doing essential back-breaking labor, with little time left over for domestic undertakings. Even as late as the 1900s, women did not have much time for quilting as pleasure. One woman told me her mother made two quilts every winter, one to use and one to put away so that she could start the next winter with at least one fresh quilt.[13] The family soon used up the quilts.

The great number of existing Missouri-German quilts date from the twentieth century with the time between the wars as the greatest reservoir. Most of these quilts derive from popular patterns. Women drew from patterns in mass magazines, shared designs from quilts in their families, and used the patterns in the German-language newspapers. These designs were usually one column wide and two to three inches long; the block design appeared but the pattern pieces were not provided. The quiltmaker was expected to be able to figure out for herself how to reproduce the design.

Mrs. Elsa Scheer of New Haven described one way patterns were passed in the early 1930s. "I saw this Broken Star in a magazine and mentioned to my mother-in-law (Mrs. John Scheer) that I had always wanted a quilt like that. She began it on my birthday and two months later gave it to me."[14] Women shared designs among themselves as well. Mrs. Herbert Kloppe of New Haven made an unusual (for Missouri-German quilts) Center Diamond quilt of white and salmon cottons for her hope chest before she married in 1938. She remembers interpreting a pattern of a quilt her sister owned.[15] Other women borrowed from newspaper designs. Mrs. Annie Hellemann of New Haven made a variation of Pickle Dish for her nephew's wedding in the thirties; she told her niece-in-law that she had taken it from a newspaper.[16] And still other women listened to the men. When Mrs. Paul Kuschel married in 1935, she made a Guiding Star for her husband. He recalled, "I loved to read and I had picked out this quilt pattern from *Capper's Weekly* long before I met my wife. I remember saying, 'If I ever get married, I hope my wife will make this quilt for me.' "[17] She did; it is still in pristine condition.

Social Significance

Families who have inherited quilts know not only the name of the maker but also the names of everyone who has owned the quilt; they proudly recite the quilt's provenance. For instance, Herbert Kloppe has an Oak Leaf, c. 1860, made by his grandmother, Louise Brune, that was passed down from Mrs. Brune to her daughter to Mr. Kloppe and will go to one of his children. Agnes Struckhoff has her grandmother's wedding quilt, and Stella Bockhous Nadler has her great-grandmother Maria Hackman Webbink's special occasion quilt which was used only at weddings, baptisms, and funerals. In each case, the family treasures the heirloom quilt, bringing it out of storage only for display and talking warmly of the woman who made it.

Many women have preserved quilts that were given to them as wedding presents and others cherish quilts as remembrances of women important to them. When Wanda Vollertsen Kropp died of double pneumonia in 1934 at the age of 33, she left four small daughters and several quilts. Each child was given one quilt by which to remember her mother.[18]

Women also made quilts as special presents for children and/or grandchildren. Before her death in 1931, Betts Theissen's mother made four Drunkard Path quilts one year as Christmas presents. She gave her daughters each a yellow-and-lavender one and her daughters-in-law each a green-and-pink one. Fred Trippe's mother made each of her five grandchildren a quilt and now his wife, Cora, is making quilts for *her* grandchildren.

The Missouri-German women also used quilts to mark special occasions. Rosemary Feldman of Dutzow has the Miniature Flower Garden her godmother, Mary Borgerding, gave her on the day of her baptism. Her parents used it in the crib in their room only on Sundays where, in turn, it covered Rosemary and her three younger siblings. They placed a matching full-sized Flower Garden on their bed; it, too, was used only on Sundays. Mrs. Harry Schiermeier owns another Sunday quilt, a crib-sized Trip Around the World, c. 1937, which was used to wrap the baby in church. (Sunday was a special day to the German women. Several spoke of quilts used only on Sunday and Mrs. Kloppe noted that she had special, embroidered pillowcases to replace the everyday ones of feed bags.)

Quilts also brought women together on sad occasions. Frieda Oelklaus' house burned in 1932 destroying the quilts she had stored in her cedar chest. When her friend, Mrs. Heitgard, heard about her loss, she brought her two quilts, a dark Nine Patch for everyday and a green-and-white for Sunday. Mrs. Oelklaus treasured both quilts for they provided not only physical warmth but also a concrete symbol of friendship.[19]

Design Characteristics

Because I was interested in quilts made before the German areas came in close contact with mainstream culture, I limited my study to quilts made before 1940. After World War II people moved frequently, the interstate highway system reduced the isolation of small towns, and St. Louisians began infiltrating the river area. Thus, the quilts in my study reflect the design tendencies of women who had only slight daily contact with the fads and fashions of the mainstream American culture.

Of the 214 quilts I recorded, the vast majority were full-sized, cotton, twentieth-century, pieced quilts. Only eight were crib-sized.

Of these, four are everyday quilts (three Nine Patch quilts and one Square Patch). The other four seem to have been celebratory quilts. Mary Borberding and her daughters Olivia Rohe and Roselind Moellering made a Miniature Flower Garden to mark the baptism of her godchild Rosemary Feldman in November, 1927. A whole-cloth crib quilt from the family of William Kiefer in Washington also appears to have been made for a christening. Made of fine quality cotton sateen and decorated with satin ribbon rosettes, it is clearly not intended for everyday use. The third quilt, a Trip Around the World, owned by Mrs. Harry Schiermeier, was designed to cover a baby in church. A much later quilt, Sunbonnet Sue, was made by Mrs. Schiermeier around 1940 for her own child.

Only two crazy quilts appeared, one in Hermann, the center of German wealth and culture, and one in New Melle, a tiny town about forty miles west of St. Louis. Nothing is known about the Hermann quilt, but the one in New Melle belongs to a Kamphoefner descendant. In the early 1900s, Hulda Kamphoefner's daughter worked as a nursemaid for the children of the chancellor of Washington University in St. Louis. She was allowed to come home once a year bringing with her the children's old clothes. From the velvets in them Hulda made her daughter a crazy quilt top. According to Alberta Toedebusch, owner of the quilt, Mrs. Kamphoefner never finished it because her daughter never married.[20] Mrs. Kamphoefner had exposure to wealth and city ways: crazy quilts are not typical of Missouri-German work.

Of the remaining 204 full-size quilts, seven are embroidered. Another sixteen are appliqued or have some applique on them. Seven of the sixteen are predominantly pieced with some applique; designs such as the North Carolina Lily which is pieced but has an applique stem or pieced flowers sitting in an appliqued pot account for five of the seven. The nine all-appliqued quilts include two Sunbonnet Sues, an Oak Leaf, a plume, four flowers, and one original cut-out design.

One hundred eighty-one (85 percent) are pieced quilts. At least in my sample, the quilt of choice is the full-sized pieced quilt.

The quilts' dominant characteristic reflects a dominant cultural characteristic of the German people; an emphasis on order. Although the quilts seem to have a great variety of designs, they are all built on a scaffolding of order in which the whole is more important

Fig. 2. Goose in the Pond *variation (c. 1900, made by Anna and Hulda Hoelcher, St. Charles) showing half and quarter blocks typical of Missouri-German quilts.*

than its parts. Quiltmakers use pattern, sets and sashing, color, and borders to emphasize the overall and to subordinate the parts.

About half the pieced quilts emphasize an all-over design. Full-size stars such as the Lone Star or the Broken Star are a particular favorite (15 quilts). Other popular all-over designs in which the individual blocks are obscured are the Wedding Ring (12 quilts) and the Irish Chain (11 quilts). Other designs, not obviously all-over, were arranged to emphasize the entire surface rather than the individual block. For instance, a Nine Patch made by Mrs. Heitgerd subordinates the block to the overall design by arranging the squares so that their background colors suggest a series of borders from the center outward. In another example, Agnes Struckhoff has played with the scale in her Single Wedding Ring so that the center block is four times the size of the regular block; it is bordered by the smaller blocks. Finally, Ida Weber's Octagon quilt is arranged in concentric circles much like a Trip Around the World. Whether flower gardens, fans, axes, or small stars, these quilts use color or arrangement to emphasize the overall and to diminish the importance of the individual block. Perhaps this emphasis on the overall explains why so few representational quilts appear. In my study I found only twenty-four (including both pieced and appliqued): twelve flower quilts, four Sunbonnets, three Fans, two Baskets, and one Oak Leaf.

The pieced quilts with clearly defined blocks are roughly divided between those put together with alternating plain blocks (sets) and those with sashing. Most of the blocks, regardless of the method of construction, are set on their points. (In fact, the point construction was so common that I was never surprised to learn that a quilt set square was made by a relative in Illinois or Kansas.)

When blocks are set on their points, there is always extra space to fill where the block meets the edge. The Germans solved this problem by using half or quarter blocks. (See Figure 2.) Sometimes, they seem to add half blocks just to fill out the size. The Pomegranate, c. 1880–1900, by Regina Hellebusch of New Haven, adds half blocks to one side. (See Figure 3.) Although this technique seems to belie the German emphasis on order, it doesn't really. The partial blocks simply continue on with the design.

The sets and sashings in the German quilts provide an important element of order. Although the quiltmaker preferred using a limited number of fabrics, she sometimes had to use a variety of scraps. When she did so, she would "hide" the scrap blocks within a strong sashing or setting which would dominate the quilt, providing a sense of order. In her Improved Nine Patch, Mrs. Louis Brandes uses such a bright yellow in the setting that it dominates the pink and blue prints of the blocks. Verna Osthoff's Wild Goose Chase has strong green sets which unify the scraps. In a typical scrap quilt, the setting or sashing is so much stronger than the blocks that it creates an overall design of its own.

Most German quilts have a clearly organized color scheme. Typically, a quilt will use two, three, or four fabrics carefully planned and repeated. The large stars have a wider variety, but they too are precisely organized. If the quiltmaker used scraps, she used enough of one color (usually bright) to hold together and order the design.

Fig. 3. Pomegranate, *c. 1880–1900, made by Regina Hellebusch, New Haven.*

More often than not, this color was a brilliant yellow or strong pink. In either case, the fabric was almost always solid rather than printed. Invariably, this fabric was the strongest color in the quilt and dominated the design. For instance, Cora Trippe's Fan quilt uses bright yellow as the handle on each fan and as an important part of the border. In the 1930s, Mabel Maeckli's mother made a Trellis in which she used squares of sharp pink and bright yellow to unify her scraps. One particularly interesting quilt, known to the family as Depression, but which looks like a Snowball, was made by Nora Hahne's mother in New Haven during the Depression. Mrs. Hahne's daughter says her grandmother tried to use up all the scraps left from earlier sewing projects in her series of Depression quilts. (She made fifteen of these quilts during 1928–1933.) She used any scrap regardless of size, shape, color or design.[21] Nevertheless, the random collection of scraps is ordered through the repetition of one yellow print, always cut in the same size triangle and recurring regularly where the blocks are joined.

Borders in the German quilts are usually very simple, often one or more bands of contrasting colors quilted in a special border pattern. Sixty-four had no borders at all while another thirty-three had borders of three inches or less. Borders made of a design, whether pieced or appliqued, are extremely rare.

Although most of the quilts with borders have them on all four sides, some have borders on only two or three sides and one, the Oak Leaf, on only one side. Mrs. Kloppe explains, "The fourth side was not finished with points or borders because when we made up the beds we put pillows over the plain side. The old quilts had small borders because beds were square, in a wooden case with a thin mattress. We didn't need large quilts."[22]

Beginning in the 1930s, some women added folded points to the outside edges of some of their quilts, especially the show quilts like Broken Star. These later quilts also have wider borders, sometimes with several bands of contrasting color.

The preferred backing was muslin, often unbleached. Many quiltmakers believed the unbleached muslin was stronger than bleached and knew it would wash out whiter and whiter.[23] Fourteen quilts have solid colored cotton backings and ten have printed cotton backings. Of the remaining quilts, three have feed sack backs (one bleached and dyed), three have wool flannel, and one has a pieced back.

All the elements of the quilt from the choice of design to the plain backing emphasize a sense of order. The quilting design plays a subordinate role. The quiltmaker chose simple quilting designs, but arranged them on the surface to mark the various elements—block, set or sashing, and border: thus the quilting subtly acknowledges the different elements of the quilt without highlighting any one of them. Commonly, the quiltmaker emphasized the block design by quilting around its pieces; sets or sashings were quilted with simple flower or geometric designs. The second most popular quilting design is a grid, either straight or skewed to make diamonds, imposed on the pieced block. Again, the sets or sashing are treated with a different quilting design. A very few quilts have an over-all quilting design which covers both the block and the set. Border designs, which are almost always different from any other quilting design used on the surface, include cables, Greek key variations, stars, fans, flowers, and feathers. When the quiltmaker used a design like a flower or feather which could be complex, she simplified it.

The more elaborate the quilt, the more elaborate the quilting design. Large stars in particular were treated to more complex quilting designs. For example, Elsa Sheer's Broken Star has rolling feathers in the corners and interlocking geometrics in the areas between the points while Viola Krueger's Broken Star has feather wreath quilting in the corners. Even these more elaborate designs, however, are subordinated to the overall design of the quilt; the quilting never calls attention to itself.

Despite the simple designs the Germans preferred, the quilting is often very finely done. Some women were justifiably proud of their skill. Anna Hoelcher Holtgraue and her twin sister Hulda Hoelcher Hackmann learned to quilt from their mother at their farm in St. Charles County in the early 1900s. When they married, they moved to neighboring farms. Although they quilted all their lives, and were in great demand at quiltings for their small, even stitches, they never invited anyone other than their mother to help them with their own quilts. None of their friends took umbrage because the sisters were acknowledged to be master quilters.[24]

Although the Missouri-German women came to quiltmaking rather late, they embraced it fervently. Their quilts differ subtly though definitely from those of their neighbors. Such regional variations bring to the study of quiltmaking a richness and depth that can lead to a greater understanding of the influences of cultural background and geographical location on quilt design. Eventually, perhaps, we will be able to piece together a reliable study of regional differences in quilts.

Notes and References:

1. William Bek, "The Followers of Duden," *Missouri Historical Review* Vol. 16 No. 2 (January, 1922), p. 379.
2. Charles van Ravenswaay, *The Arts and Architecture of German Settlements in Missouri.* (Columbia, Missouri: University of Missouri Press, 1977), pp. 14–15.
3. Interview with Clara Kuschel, New Haven, July, 1982.
4. van Ravenswaay, p. 70.
5. *Ibid.*, p. 452.
6. *Ibid.*, p. 447.
7. Interview with Elsa Scheer, New Haven, July, 1982.
8. William Bek, "The Followers of Duden," *Missouri Historical Review* Vol. 16 No. 3 (April, 1922), p. 345.
9. Interview with Gertrude Allgeyer, Rhineland, August, 1983.
10. Interview with Mrs. Herbert Kloppe, New Haven, September, 1983.
11. Communication of Agnes Struckhoff, Augusta, October, 1983.
12. Interview with Ralph Gregory, Washington, June, 1982. For weather conditions, see Gottfried Duden, *Report on a Journey to the Western States of North America,* ed. by James W. Goodrich (Columbia, Missouri: University of Missouri Press, 1980), pp. 58, 65, 80, 161–162.
13. Interview with Dorothy Meinerschagan, Augusta, June, 1982.
14. Interview with Elsa Scheer, New Haven, July, 1982.
15. Interview with Mrs. Herbert Kloppe, New Haven, September, 1982.
16. Communication from Mrs. Andreas J. Meyer, New Haven, September, 1983.
17 Interview with Paul Kuschel, New Haven, July, 1982.
18. Communication from Mrs. Florence Meyer, Hermann, June, 1982.
19. Interview with Frieda Oelklaus, St. Charles, August, 1982.
20. Interview with Alberta Toedebusch, New Melle, August, 1982.
21. Communication from Nora Hahne, New Haven, September, 1983.
22. Interview with Mrs. Herbert Kloppe, New Haven, September, 1982.
23. *Ibid.*
24. Interview with Frieda Oelklaus, St. Charles, May, 1982.

*I am grateful to the American Association of University Women for providing the grant which made this research possible.

Quilts Cited

1. Four Patch, c. 1912. Made and owned by Gertrude Allgeyer, Rhineland.
2. North Carolina Lily, c. 1858. Made by Agnes Struckhoff's grandmother. Owned by Agnes Struckhoff, Augusta.
3. Broken Star, c. 1930. Made by Mrs. John Scheer, New Haven. Owned by Elsa Scheer Wehmeyer, New Haven.
4. Center Diamond, 1936. Made and owned by Mrs. Herbert Kloppe, New Haven.
5. Pickle Dish variation, c. 1930. Made by Annie Hellemann. Owned by Mrs. Andreas J. Meyer, New Haven.
6. Guiding Star, 1935. Made by Clara Kuschel. Owned by Paul Kuschel, New Haven.
7. Oak Leaf, c. 1860. Made by Louise Brune. Owned by Herbert Kloppe, New Haven.
8. Drunkard's Path, c. 1930. Made by Katherine Yoest. Owned by Betts Theissen, Rhineland.
9. Miniature Flower Garden, 1927. Made by Mary Borgerding and her daughters, Olivia Rohe and Roselind Moellering. Owned by Rosemary Feldman, Dutzow.
10. Flower Garden, c. 1930. Maker unknown. Owned by Rosemary Feldman, Dutzow.
11. Trip Around the World, 1927. Maker unknown. Owned by Mrs. Harry Schiermeier, New Melle.
12. Nine Patch, c. 1930. Made by Mrs. Heitgerd. Owned by Frieda Oelklaus, St. Charles.
13. Crib-sized quilts:

    Nine Patch, c. 1910. Maker unknown. Owned by Alberta Toedebusch, New Melle.

    Nine Patch, c. 1920. Made and owned by Marie Koch, Washington.

    Nine Patch, c. 1900. Made by member of the family of Ida Weber. Owned by Ervin Von Behren, New Haven.

    Square Patch, c. 1920. Made by a member of the family of Ida Weber. Owned by Ervin Von Behren.

    Whole-cloth crib quilt, c. 1920. Made by member of family of William Kiefer, Washington. Owned by the author.

    Sunbonnet Sue, c. 1940. Made and owned by Mrs. Harry Schiermeier, New Melle.
14. Crazy Quilt, c. 1880. Maker unknown. Collection of Brush and Palette Club, Hermann.

15. Crazy Quilt, c. 1910. Made by Hulda Kamphoefner. Owned by Alberta Toedebusch, New Melle.
16. Single Wedding Ring, c. 1938. Made and owned by Agnes Struckhoff, Augusta.
17. Octagon, c. 1910. Made by member of family of Ida Weber. Owned by Ervin Von Behren, New Haven.
18. Pomegranate, c. 1880–1890. Made by Regina Hellebusch, New Haven. Owned by the author.
19. Improved Nine Patch, c. 1930. Made by Mrs. Louis Brandes. Owned by Virginia Auping, New Melle.
20. Wild Goose Chase, 1936. Made and owned by Verna Osthoff, Defiance.
21. Fan, c. 1930. Designed and owned by Cora Trippe, Holstein.
22. Trellis, c. 1930. Made by Martha Maupin, Washington. Owned by her daughter, Mabel Maeckli, New Haven.
23. Depression, c. 1929. Made by Nora Hahne's mother, Washington. Owned by Nora Hahne, New Haven.
24. Broken Star, c. 1930. Made and owned by Viola Krueger.

Kansas City Star Quilt Patterns

Louise O. Townsend

"Kansas City Stars" are a remarkable body of quilt patterns which appeared in the three *Kansas City Star* newspapers for about thirty years—roughly the '30s, '40s, and '50s of this century. Unlike the syndicated quilt columns of the period—such as Florence LaGanke's "Nancy Page Quilt Club" which appeared in newspapers from coast to coast[1]—the Kansas City Stars emanated from one regional source, and they were disseminated to quiltmakers in an eight-state section of the country over a given period of time. They offer a basis for studying the quilt pattern preferences of the midwest region as well as creating a means of dating and naming quilts from this area during one thirty-year period.

The *Kansas City Star* organization was founded in the late 1800s with William Rockhill Nelson as its publisher. There was a morning paper called the *Kansas City Times* in which few, if any, quilt patterns appeared. The afternoon paper, the *Kansas City Star*, carried quilt patterns, usually in the Saturday edition, or every night of the week if a series pattern was in progress. These patterns in the local *Kansas City Star* began to appear in September of 1928 and continued until about June of 1937 when they became more sporadic, and then didn't appear at all. Local quiltmakers probably did not object to this disappearance because in 1933 the *Star* began an almost daily series of mail-order patterns through its needlecraft department.

The patterns found in the local *Kansas City Star* on Saturday nights were repeated the following Wednesday in the *Weekly Kansas City Star*.[2] This newspaper billed itself as the "largest farmers' weekly in America" with a circulation in 1931 of 490,000 paid subscribers.[3] As a major midwestern farm journal, the *Weekly Kansas City Star* had three mailing editions: the Missouri Edition which was mailed

Louise O. Townsend: 531 Franklin St, Denver, CO 80218

to subscribers in Missouri and Iowa; the Kansas Edition which went
to persons in Kansas, Nebraska, and Colorado; and the Arkansas/
Oklahoma Edition which was sent to those two states plus Texas.
Thus, an eight-state area received the *Weekly Kansas City Star*. Quilt
patterns in this weekly newspaper began in 1928 when the local
paper first began to carry them, and continued into the 1950s.

Sometimes only one or two of the mailing editions of the *Weekly
Kansas City Star* would carry a quilt pattern. An example is The Sea
Shell Quilt which appeared only in the Arkansas/Oklahoma Edition on July 28, 1948.[4] If you were a collector in Kansas or Nebraska
or Iowa, you would be unlikely to have a copy of this pattern in
your collection. If you received the local *Kansas City Star*, you would
not have collected as many patterns as someone in Nebraska or
Arkansas, because they were collecting from the *Weekly Kansas City
Star* which carried patterns for more years than the local paper did.
On the other hand, collectors of the *Weekly Kansas City Star* patterns probably had very few of the mail-order patterns and none of
the four "series" quilt patterns presented in the *Star* because these
appeared almost exclusively in the local newspaper. An example is
the 1930 Memory Bouquet series which appeared in the local *Kansas
City Star* only, with admonitions to the reader to save the patterns
as there would be no mailed patterns. The *Weekly Kansas City Star*
during the same period carried three single patterns—The Spider
Web, The Marble Floor, and Pin Wheel—with no mention at all
about the series quilt being given in the local newspaper.

After 1937 there were some weeks when no quilt pattern at all appeared in the *Kansas City Star* or the *Weekly Kansas City Star*. In
1938, for example, there were only 32 quilt patterns presented all
year; by 1946 there were just 18. Sometimes embroidery designs for
huck toweling, cookie cutter designs, stencil designs, or other hand-
work would be substituted for a quilt pattern, and undoubtedly
some of these designs were used on regional quilts.

By the early 1950s the *Weekly Kansas City Star* became known as
the *Weekly Star Farmer*. Patterns that can be identified as coming
from the *Kansas City Star* or from the *Weekly Kansas City Star* appeared between 1928 and 1951. After 1951 they were really *Weekly
Star Farmer* patterns—from the same newspaper company, and with
the same illustrator, but with a new newspaper masthead.[5]

The Kansas City Star patterns can be divided according to the newspapers in which they appeared, but they are also interesting to consider by designer or illustrator. The term "illustrator" is often preferable to "designer" because in reality a large portion of the Kansas City Stars were older, traditional patterns or new ideas sent in by reader contributors. The three women who illustrated them over the years probably did not "design" very many of these patterns, but rather "illustrated" traditional patterns or contemporary designs from reader contributions or from other sources.

One of the most surprising things about the "Kansas City Stars" is that the McKim Studios label is on so few of them—about 75 altogether. Ruby Short McKim, who was born in Millersburg, Illinois, in 1891, moved to Independence, Missouri, a suburb of Kansas City, when she was ten years old.[6] Because she lived nearby, we have a tendency to assume that she was *the* quilt lady at the *Kansas City Star*. However, she was also the art/needlework editor for *Better Homes and Gardens* magazine, and a cofounder of the Kimport Doll Company in Independence. With her husband, Arthur McKim, she designed and sold many newspaper features including the quilt patterns. The two also developed a forerunner of today's comic strips with puzzles, stories, and pictures for children. Almost all of Mrs. McKim's well known quilt patterns, especially the "series" patterns, appeared in her own publications, or in newspapers other than the *Kansas City Star*. Some examples of her work include parts of the "Prudence Penny" quilt column in the *Seattle Post-Intelligencer*[7] and her Flower Garden series shown in the *Indianapolis Star*[8] and other newspapers.

McKim Studios provided the first quilt pattern in the *Kansas City Star*—The Pine Tree on September 22, 1928[9]—and McKim patterns continued for almost two years, until July 26, 1930.[10] If a Kansas City Star with a McKim Studios byline can be dated later than this, it is a repeat of one of the 75 McKim patterns published during the first two years of Kansas City Star patterns.

Ruby McKim was primarily a designer/illustrator and made very few quilts herself. However, she always had one quilt made up from each design to see how it would work. McKim patterns usually gave at least one color combination if not several, and suggested the layout for the quilt, telling how many blocks would be needed for certain sizes of finished quilts. Among the early patterns, there were suggestions on how to make cardboard templates, how to piece in

sequence,[11] and information on how to file the designs by placing all
of the pieces for one pattern into an envelope and pasting the block
sketch on the outside.[12] Unlike her successors at the *Star*, it was
obvious that Ruby McKim knew what hazards might face a novice
who had no other available instructions except the weekly quilt
patterns in the newspaper.

By the middle of 1930 McKim's quilt patterns disappeared from
the *Kansas City Star*, although they continued to be seen in many
other newspapers across the country. In 1931 her book *One Hundred
One Patchwork Patterns* was published, and she was busy throughout
the period with her "Designs Worth Doing" mail-order business.

The new quilt pattern illustrator was Eveline (pronounced Eva-
leen) Foland whose first pattern, Broken Circle or Sunflower, had
appeared in the local paper on March 23, 1929.[13] Her patterns were
interspersed with McKim's work until mid-1930 when they began
appearing exclusively, every week, until late in 1932. Little is known
about Mrs. Foland's personal life other than her maiden name of
Smith, and her husband's first name, Jimmy.[14] She had been working for the *Star* as an illustrator since the mid-twenties, usually pre-
paring sketches for the fashion, home, or society pages of the
newspaper.

In the twenties there were few photographs in newspapers, so
Mrs. Foland or another of the paper's illustrators would be sent to a
private home to sketch the wedding gown of a local bride for the
society column,[15] or to the Better Homes Exposition to illustrate the
newest in home furnishings.[16] The *Weekly Kansas City Star* carried
mail-order dress patterns called "Georgette Patterns," and Eveline
Foland's name appeared on many of these illustrations in the late
twenties.[17]

After she left the *Star* at the end of 1932, Mrs. Foland taught
fashion art at the Jane Hayes Gates Institute in Kansas City, and she
continued to do free-lance fashion ads for local department stores.[18]
Her name was no longer connected with quilt pattern illustration
although an occasional pattern in the *Star* would bear her bold signature. These were invariably repeats of her patterns published between 1929 and 1932.

There were 131 individual patterns signed by Eveline Foland which
appeared in the *Star*. A few of these were repeats—such as Tennessee
Star which appeared both in January and September of 1931.[19] Some

of Mrs. Foland's pattern captions indicated that they had been sketched at a local home or at a local quilt show. Ararat, a pieced elephant pattern dated June 6 and 10, 1931, was named for the elephant in Kansas City's Swope Park Zoo.[20] A few weeks after this pattern appeared in the paper, Foland created Giddap, a pieced donkey which was requested by the Ladies' Aid at the Sedalia, Missouri, Congregational Church, because the ladies wanted to be well prepared for the political conventions and presidential campaign of 1932.[21]

Mrs. Foland was the illustrator and probably also the designer of three of the four "series" quilt patterns that appeared in the *Kansas City Star*. In late 1929 her first series for an embroidered quilt called Santa's Parade in a Nursery Quilt appeared nightly for twelve nights (rather than the more usual once-per-week offering of patterns).[22] Only two of these patterns, the ones that had appeared in the Saturday edition of the local paper, were given in the *Weekly Kansas City Star*, and their new captions did not mention the rest of the series.[23]

Foland's second and third series quilt designs were companion pieces well suited for embroidery or very fine applique.[24] The twenty-part Memory Bouquet appeared in October and November of 1930,[25] and the eighteen designs for the Horn of Plenty Quilt were offered in January and February of 1932.[26] These two series patterns appeared only in the local *Kansas City Star*, though one of them, Memory Bouquet, was also sold to the *Detroit News* as The Flower Garden Quilt. It appeared in that newspaper in 1931–32, the only known appearance of Foland's work in a newspaper other than the *Kansas City Star*.[27]

Memory Bouquet is quite similar to Ruby McKim's Flower Garden series which appeared in the *Indianapolis Star* and other newspapers of the period.[28] Foland's pattern included 20 different flowers, each arranged in a green bowl and placed on a 9″ x 12″ piece of muslin. Blocks were separated by 4″-wide green sashes, and there was a tulip with three leaves for a border design to finish the quilt. A year after the patterns appeared in the newspaper, the *Star* printed a photo of a finished Memory Bouquet quilt made by Miss Doris Foster of Gilman City, Missouri.[29]

Mrs. Foland's third series, The Horn of Plenty Quilt, appeared in 1932. The captions for the 18 fruit patterns gave very specific color suggestions for the embroidery and applique, and there was a special horn-of-plenty quilting design, a border treatment, and a diagram of the finished quilt.

One other series quilt appeared in the *Star* about the time of Mrs. Foland's departure in 1932. It was called The Happy Childhood Quilt for Good Children and included 12 toy patterns with a 13th Christmas tree design that was used between the toy blocks.[30] It was to be done in applique with heavy use of bias tape, and its designer was Aileen Bullard who apparently was not employed by the *Kansas City Star*. These patterns were the only ones in the *Star* with Bullard's byline, and they were copyrighted by Cox Features rather than by the *Star*, so they were probably purchased by the newspaper when it found itself in disarray at the imminent departure of Eveline Foland from its staff in late 1932.

On December 17 and 21, 1932, Mrs. Foland's Pilot's Wheel pattern appeared in the *Star*, but it is likely that she had already left the staff. The pattern pieces were shown along with a caption that stated "This will not be an easy block to piece...." But the pattern sketch was missing, and there must have been a flurry of protest letters inquiring about the assembly of the 37 pieces, because on February 25 and March 1, 1933, the Pilot's Wheel pattern was repeated, this time with a block sketch and a fancily lettered title.

After The Star of Hope pattern appeared on December 31, 1932 and January 4, 1933, there were no more regular Eveline Foland patterns in the *Kansas City Star*. The newspaper now had to draw upon the services of Edna Marie Dunn. Only four patterns appeared with Miss Dunn's signature,[31] but she was the anonymous illustrator of the *Star's* quilt patterns from the beginning of 1933 until she retired from the paper in 1964.[32] In reality, the least known of the *Star's* three quilt pattern illustrators was the most important one, for her patterns provided a steady stream of design ideas for midwestern quiltmakers for thirty years.

Miss Dunn was born in Chicago in 1893, but came to Kansas City at the age of seven. After returning to Chicago to train at its Academy of Art, she worked as a free-lance advertising illustrator for Harzfelds, Woolf Brothers, and Rothchild's department stores in Kansas City. In 1922 she won a competition for selecting a fashion artist for the *Kansas City Star* and she commenced a routine that would last for 45 years "without missing a deadline." Though someone else's work would appear during the month of August — her vacation time — Miss Dunn produced a fashion sketch for each day's newspaper edition, with several sketches for the women's section of the Sunday paper. Beginning in 1933, she added the once-per-week quilt pattern illustration to her list of duties at the *Star.*

Edna Marie Dunn did not make quilts, and thus her patterns for the *Star* should be classified as illustrations and not as original designs. Most were reader-contributed patterns, and often the caption would state the contributor's name. Readers sent pattern ideas to the *Star* both on paper and in completed fabric form. Sometimes a copy of a pattern from an earlier edition of the *Star* was sent in, and then a McKim Studios or an Eveline Foland pattern would be repeated. Sometimes an earlier pattern was contributed, and Miss Dunn just renamed it and added a new caption. For example, her own first pattern for the *Star* was Interlocked Squares on September 10 and 14, 1932. It was repeated on January 28, 1948; in the *Weekly Kansas City Star* with a new title, A Four-Part Strip Quilt.

Some patterns were copied from quilts handed down in a reader's family, or seen at a friend's home. If the contributor didn't know the name of the pattern, Miss Dunn created one unless she found the design quickly in some other source. Usually she was too busy with her fashion illustration work to spend much time researching quilt names or designing quilt patterns.

Since the *Weekly Kansas City Star* was mailed to eight surrounding states, the contributed patterns came from a wide area, and sometimes they were named for local landmarks, such as Hazel Valley Crossroads[33] named for the contributor's hometown in Arkansas, or Sandhills Star[34] named for a large area in western Nebraska. The 1936 presidential campaign brought a display of regional pride for Kansas's native son, Alf Landon, the Republican candidate for President of the United States. The *Star* published The Landon Sunflower[35] and Peggy Anne's Special[36] named for Landon's daughter. Several patterns to honor the Red Cross appeared during the World War II years,[37] and midwestern concerns about this war were reflected in reader-contributed patterns with names like The Army Star, Roads to Berlin, and The Victory Boat.[38]

The reader-contributors of quilt patterns for the *Kansas City Star* were generally women, though several times a pattern was contributed by a child[39]—usually the daughter of an avid quilter—or by a man.[40] Some designs were sent in by people whom we now consider to be among the great quiltmakers of the century. Mrs. A.B. Snyder of Flats, Nebraska, contributed the <u>Semi-Circle Saw</u> on July 3, 1946, and <u>Return of the Swallows</u> on October 2, 1946. Today, we immediately recognize that contributor as Grace Snyder of North Platte, Nebraska, and we remember her <u>Return of the Swallows</u> quilt made in 1944, and now in the collection of her daughter, Nellie Snyder Yost.[41]

Many of the reader-contributors were also pattern collectors. By 1941 Mrs. Dayton D. Noel of Unionville, Missouri, had 350 illustrations since she had been "collecting quilt block patterns and designs for homemade articles reproduced in the *Weekly Star* [since 1928]."[42] Mrs. Ed Martin of New Home Farm, Gravette, Arkansas, also had a collection of *Weekly Star* patterns. The caption under her contribution of <u>Arkansas Cross Roads</u>, dated in 1941, said that "For the last ten years she has pasted them into a big book that she says 'money couldn't buy!' "[43]

Another source of quilt patterns for local *Kansas City Star* readers was the almost daily mail-order advertisements that began in 1933. From February 20 until May 25, 1933, these were ordered from the Kansas City Star Quilt Service, although the patterns actually came from Home Art Studio in Des Moines, Iowa.[44] The advertisements were discontinued in May but there must have been many inquiries because in October of the same year a new mail-order service, The Kansas City Star Needlecraft Department, began. At first the mailing address for this service was Kansas City, Missouri; later it changed to Chicago, Illinois; and by 1945 it changed again to New York City. When one received a pattern in the mail, the return address was for The Kansas City Star Needlecraft Department, but the envelope and pattern inside were clearly marked as Laura Wheeler Designs.[45] None of these mail-order patterns was directly connected with the *Kansas City Star*, and the newspaper carried only a tiny sketch of the quilt pattern to be ordered. However, a few of them later found their way into the weekly quilt patterns illustrated by Edna Marie Dunn whenever they were contributed by a reader.

The quilt patterns in the *Kansas City Star* and the *Weekly Kansas City Star* were often the only source of new designs for quiltmakers in the Midwest of the 1930s and '40s. There were very few books available, although the *Star* did review two important ones from the period: Ruth Finley's *Old Patchwork Quilts and the Women Who*

Made Them in 1929,[46] and Hall and Kretsinger's *The Romance of the Patchwork Quilt in America* in 1935.[47] In the *Star* itself, there were very few informative articles on quilting. One in April of 1929 was titled "Quilting on Your Sewing Machine,"[48] and another in 1934 showed a diagram and gave directions for "An Easily Made and Compact Quilting Frame."[49] But other than Ruby McKim's few, brief directions in captions of some of her weekly quilt patterns from 1928–1930, there was little in the newspaper to explain how quilts were made.

But quilts *were* made! The *Star* covered quilt shows in the area, many of which were held in churches and sponsored by the Ladies' Aid Society or the Women's Circle. Sometimes there would be displays by the sewing circle of the Order of Eastern Star, or by a chapter of the Women's Relief Corps.[50] Once in a while a Professional Women's Club would hold a quilt show—one in Bucklin, Kansas (in the southwest part of the state), was held in 1931 and displayed 147 quilts from that one small community.[561] A woman named Elma Eaton Karr gave many public lectures on quilts, and these were always well attended. The *Star* reported one at the First Baptist Church on Linwood Boulevard in Kansas City in 1934 which brought together 400 women and an exhibit of 140 quilts.[52]

The Better Homes Exposition, held annually in Kansas City in February, also attracted a huge outpouring of quilts. In 1932 the show's directors hoped to attract at least 100 quilts for an area in the northwest corner of the Kansas City Convention Hall. However, they had to close the contest at 300 entries when they ran out of space. (The prize for the best quilt in that show was a marble-topped coffee table.)[53]

The Jones Store, a major department store in Kansas City, also held an annual contest during the thirties. In October of 1931, one of their ads proclaimed "634 Quilts Entered in Our Quilt Fair!" on the first floor of the Walnut Street store.[54] During the three-day show, the customers were the judges of the five top prizewinners, so winners were not announced until the end of the show. The idea, of course, was to pull in customers to buy quilting supplies in the store.

Newspaper accounts of these shows—whether they were held in a church, at a department store, or at the Better Homes Exposition— often noted that many of the quilts in the show were made from patterns seen in recent years in the *Kansas City Star*. The weekly quilt patterns were a major source of inspiration for quiltmakers in the eight-state region.

Edna Marie Dunn was the illustrator during most of the years when quilt patterns appeared in the *Kansas City Star.* Her job was to redraft and illustrate the designs submitted by readers, so she and the newspaper became a mechanism for quilt pattern exchange among midwestern quiltmakers. Readers sent designs to the newspaper which Miss Dunn illustrated, and they copied the designs submitted by others for their own quilts. The patterns were clipped and saved by hundreds of quiltmakers, and many of these collections have been handed down within families of quiltmakers, and have been so highly prized by the collector or keeper of family treasures that they reappear outside of the eight-state region when they have been carried intact with other household goods and personal belongings to a new location. Other quilt fanciers who live outside of the *Kansas City Star* region, or who do not have an inherited collection to enjoy, can still use these patterns today as several contemporary publishers have reprinted groups of them. As well, many collections have been discovered in garage and· antique sales—ready to inspire a whole new generation of American quiltmakers.

Notes and References:

1. The "Nancy Page Quilt Club" was copyrighted by Publisher's Syndicate and among the newspaper clippings in the author's collection are patterns published in the *Indianapolis Star*, the *Dayton Daily News* (Ohio), the *Buffalo Times* (New York), the *Peoria Star* (Illinois), and the *Semi-Weekly Farm News* (Dallas, Texas). The contributors to the column were from such widely diverse places as Fairfield, Connecticut; Stockton, California; Etna, New Hampshire; Meadville, Georgia; Mabank, Texas; Orofino, Idaho; and Whitby, Ontario, which suggests the widespread readership of this syndicated quilt column. It is interesting to note that very few contributions to the "Nancy Page Quilt Club" came from the eight-state region served by the *Kansas City Star* (KCS).

2. The first 13 quilt patterns appeared in *KCS* on the Saturday *after* they had appeared in the *Weekly Kansas City Star* (WKCS). In mid-December of 1928, the order was reversed to Saturday/Wednesday, and continued until patterns disappeared from the local paper. Unless otherwise noted, all references to patterns which include dates refer to the Saturday/Wednesday order — *KCS/WKCS*.

3. Advertisement, *WKCS* (Oklahoma, Arkansas Edition), Wednesday, September 16, 1931, p. 7. The ad also mentioned that 66% of Kansas subscribers and 68% of Missouri subscribers were farm families.

4. *WKCS* (Oklahoma/Arkansas Edition), Wednesday, July 28, 1948, p. 3. The caption stated that the pattern was from the original needlework designs of Mrs. Margaret King of Salem, Arkansas.

5. In May of 1961 the *Weekly Star Farmer* merged with the *Missouri Ruralist* and *Kansas Farmer*. The last edition of the *Weekly Star Farmer* on May 24, 1961, carried the last "Kansas City Star" pattern, A Fan of Many Colors, on p. 6. (This information was kindly shared with the author by Carol Crabb.)

6. Biographical information about Ruby Short McKim was obtained from her obituary which appeared in the *Kansas City Times*, Thursday, July 29, 1976, p. 7D, and from "Ruby Short McKim: A Memorial," *Quilter's Newsletter Magazine* No. 86, December 1976, p. 14.

7. Examples in the author's collection include several of "Prudence Penny's Album Quilt" with the McKim Studios signature. These examples are undated.

8. McKim's Flower Garden Quilt was presented as a contest for Hoosiers in the *Indianapolis Star*, with patterns appearing once a week beginning on November 11, 1929. "Quilters, On Your Marks ... Go!" The *Indianapolis Star*, Sunday, September 25, 1976, Section 7, p. 11.

126 KC STAR PATTERNS

9. *KCS*, Saturday, September 22, 1928, p. F-16. This pattern had already appeared in the previous *WKCS*, Wednesday, September 19, 1928, p. 7.
10. Clay's Choice, *KCS*, Saturday, July 27, 1930, p. F-13. Repeated in *WKCS*, Wednesday, July 30, 1930, p. 9.
11. Instructions for making a cardboard pattern and piecing in sequence were given with the pattern, The Rambler, December 29, 1928, and January 2, 1929.
12. Instructions for saving patterns were given with the pattern Spider Web, January 19 and 23, 1929.
13. *KCS*, Saturday, March 23, 1929, p. F-15. The pattern appeared in *WKCS* on Wednesday, March 27, 1929, p. 7.
14. Information about Eveline Foland was obtained from phone interviews by Barbara Brackman with Marguerite Weaver of Independence, Missouri, and Jack and Clara Tillotson of Kansas City, Missouri, and reported to the author in a letter dated October 24, 1980.
15. "A Christmas Bride Chooses White Satin and Duchess lace," *KCS*, Friday, December 25, 1931, p. 18; and "A Bridal Gown of Satin is Innocent of Any Ornamentation," *KCS*, Thursday, February 4, 1932, p. 9.
16. "A Corner of the Children's Room at the Better Homes Show," *KCS*, Wednesday, February 26, 1930, p. 12, and "The Fireplace from the Wayside Inn at Better Home Show," *KCS*, Thursday, February 29, 1930, p. 15.
17. "New Georgette Patterns for Spring Sewing," *WKCS*, Wednesday, February 13, 1929, p. 7. This is just one example of these patterns which Mrs. Foland illustrated throughout 1929.
18. Letter to the author from Marguerite Weaver, dated March 1, 1983.
19. The pattern for Tennessee Star given on January 10 and 14, 1931, said that the quilt block would be 10″ square, while the same pattern given on September 12 and 16, 1931, did not mention the size. Otherwise, the two patterns are identical.
20. Ararat the elephant was a Kansas City favorite for many years, and his photo appeared frequently in the newspaper. An item in *KCS*, Sunday, August 9, p. 8A, mentioned that his quarters in the Swope Park Zoo had received a new paint job. In the Sunday paper on May 21, 1944, p. 1C, there was a photo of Ararat who was now 34 years old and weighed 4,000 pounds.
21. Giddap appeared in *KCS* on Saturday, July 18, 1931, p. E-13, and in *WKCS* on Wednesday, July 22, 1931, p. 6.
22. Santa's Parade in a Nursery Quilt included the following patterns (given in consecutive order): *Old Woman Who Lived in a Shoe, The*

Dish that Ran Away with the Spoon, Punch and Judy, Little Crystal [a fairy], *Old King Cole, Humpty Dumpty, Jack-in-the-Box, Three Men in a Tub, The Three Bears, Old Mother Goose, The Little Wooden Soldier,* and *Old Santa Himself.* These patterns appeared between Tuesday, December 10, and Sunday, December 22, 1919, in *KCS.*

23. Old King Cole and The Little Wooden Soldier appeared in *WKCS* as single patterns with captions that made no reference to the series appearing in the local *KCS.* They appeared on December 18 and 25, 1929, respectively.

24. "Something About the Horn of Plenty Quilt," *KCS*, Monday, January 4, 1932, p. 8, mentions that this quilt is "the sister and sequel to the Memory Bouquet Quilt." Once again there was the admonition that "No back numbers can be reprinted," so the reader was advised to clip and save all of the patterns.

25. Memory Bouquet included the following patterns (given in consecutive order): *Iris, Hollyhock, Tulip, Canterbury Bell, Bleeding Heart, Violet, Carnation, Hyacinth, Double Rose, Zinnia, Primrose, Geranium, Black-Eyed Susan, Morning Glory, Holly, Petunia, Lily-of-the-Valley, Wild Rose, Jonquil, Cosmos,*and *Border Design.* These patterns appeared between Monday, October 13, and Friday, November 7, 1930.

26. The Horn of Plenty Quilt included the following patterns (given in consecutive order): *Apple, Apricot, Cherry, Blue Plum, Lemon, Grape, Banana, Peach, Orange, Pomegranate, Currants, Kumquat, Cranberry, Damson Plum, Loganberry, Yellow Apple, Avocado Pear, Strawberry, Quilting Design, Diagram of the Quilt,* and *Border Design.* These patterns appeared between Tuesday, January 5, and Friday, February 26, 1932.

27. Illustrations for The Flower Garden Quilt in the *Detroit News* looked exactly the same as those for The Memory Bouquet which appeared in *KCS,* although some of the copy was different. The *Detroit News* carried the 22 patterns approximately every week beginning October 14, 1931, and continuing until April 20, 1932.

28. For purposes of comparison with note 24, McKim's Flower Garden Quilt contained the following patterns: *Lilac, Daffodil, Tulip, Iris, Nasturtium, Poppy, Canterbury (Blue) Bells, Rose, Lily-of-the-Valley, Carnation, Chinese Lantern Pod, Bleeding Heart, Daisy, Sweet Pea, Tiger Lily, Cosmos, Water Lily, Hollyhock, Geranium, Delphinium, Trumpet Vine, Petunia, Zinnia, Chrysanthemum,* and *Pansy.* Foland's patterns appeared in *KCS* less than a year after the McKim patterns appeared in the *Indianapolis Star.*

29. "*The Memory Bouquet Quilt* Returns to the *Star* in its Completed Form," *KCS*, Thursday, June 25, 1931, p. 11. The photo caption also

says that Miss Foster used six spools of cotton and two months of spare time to complete the quilt.

30. The Happy Childhood Quilt for Good Children included the following patterns (given in consecutive order): *Layout of Quilt, Tree, Ball, Rag Doll, Moving Toy* [car], *Tricycle, Beads, Sled, Train Engine, Teddy Bear, Building Blocks, Wagon, Boat,* and *Doll Carriage.* These patterns appeared between Monday, October 31, and Saturday, November 19, 1932. The Tree pattern was given in *WKCS* on Wednesday, November 16, 1932, and the quilt layout was given on Wednesday, November 23, 1932. Neither of these patterns mentioned the series in the local paper, and the quilt layout was accompanied by a caption that said, "You make your own patterns.... Good luck."

31. The four patterns with Edna Marie Dunn's signature were: Interlocked Squares, September 10 and 14, 1932; The Arkansas Star, January 14 and 18, 1933; Bouquet in a Fan, March 18 and 22, 1933; and Morning Glory, December 23 and 27, 1933.

32. Information about Edna Marie Dunn's life and her work as quilt pattern illustrator for the *KCS* was obtained in an interview by the author with Mrs. Frank Douglass (née: Edna Marie Dunn) in Lee's Summit, Missouri, in February of 1978, and through correspondence between the author and Miss Dunn's niece, Shirley Mikesell, also of Lee's Summit, from February through May of 1978. See also "The Meetin' Place: Let is untroduce you to Edna Marie Dunn of Kansas City, Missouri," *Quilter's Newsletter Magazine* No. 107, November/December 1978, p. 14.

33. Hazel Valley Crossroads, October 6 and 10, 1934, sent in by 12-year-old Freda Napier.

34. Sandhills Star, *WKCS*, Wednesday, January 18, 1939, sent in by Myrtle Timblin Ogden of Lamar, Nebraska.

35. The Landon Sunflower, September 12 and 16, 1936, sent by Mrs. H.E. Meyers of Cherokee, Kansas.

36. Peggy Anne's Special, October 3 and 14, 1936, sent in by Mrs. A.B. Eiver of Waverly, Kansas.

37. In all, six different Red Cross patterns appeared in *KCS* in the '30s and '40s. They were: Red Cross Quilt, April 16 and 20, 1932 (repeated as The Red Cross in *WKCS*, Wednesday, September 27, 1939, and as A Red-White-Blue Color Scheme, Wednesday, January 13, 1943); The Red Cross, July 21 and 25, 1934; The Red Cross Quilt, Wednesday, January 22, 1941; The Red Cross Quilt, Wednesday, October 28, 1942, The Red Cross Quilt, Wednesday, January 15, 1947; and A Red and White Crisscross, Wednesday, September 9, 1942.

38. The Army Star, Wednesday, May 26, 1943; Roads to Berlin, Wednesday, September 13, 1944; and The Victory Boat, Wednesday, September 27, 1944.

39. Some examples of patterns sent in by children include: The Dog Quilt, May 2 and 6, 1936, "by a girl in her early teens"; The Airport, July 11 and 15, 1936, by 14-year-old Muriel Clift of Mammoth Springs, Arkansas; and The Pin-Wheel, April 7 and 11, 1934, by 11-year-old Mary Newton of Denison, Texas.

40. Some examples of patterns sent in by men include: Hidden Star, July 4 and 8, 1936, by Mr. R. Prier of Purdy, Missouri; Happy Hunting Grounds, October 10 and 21, 1936, by Lloyd Krober of Piedmont, Oklahoma; and A Young Man's Invention, February 29 and March 4, 1936, "drawn by a young man during the Civil War for his grandmother."

41. Mrs. Snyder's quilt was 69″ x 82½″, and somewhat different from the sketch made of it for the newspaper by Edna Marie Dunn. See Plate 46, *Quilts from Nebraska Collections*, a catalog of a quilt exhibition at the Sheldon Memorial Art Gallery, University of Nebraska-Lincoln, September 17 to October 13, 1974.

42. From the caption for Anna's Choice, *WKCS*, Wednesday, February 26, 1941.

43. From the caption for The Arkansas Cross Roads, *WKCS*, Wednesday, March 19, 1941.

44. The numbers assigned to the Kansas City Star Quilt Service patterns match those used by Home Art Studios. Two of the items other than quilt patterns which were offered during the series ("Master Quilting Album" on Friday, April 24, 1933, and "Colonial Quilt Booklet" on Tuesday, February 28, 1933) can also be attributed to Home Art Studios.

45. An example in the author's collection is an envelope and pattern clearly marked both "Kansas City Star Needlecraft Department" and "Laura Wheeler Designs," which were mailed to Mrs. C. M. Richardson, 933 Indiana Street, Lawrence, Kansas. The mailing label has the number 469 on it, corresponding to the Palm pattern inside, which was advertised in *KCS* on Friday, January 12, 1934, and again on Tuesday, September 18, 1934.

46. "The Patchwork Quilt Gets Into a Book," *KCS*, Friday, November 8, 1929, p. 31.

47. "A New Book on Quilts," *KCS*, Wednesday, September 4, 1935, p. 14.

48. "Quilting on Your Sewing Machine," *KCS*, Tuesday, April 23, 1929, p. 13.

49. "An Easily Made and Compact Quilting Frame," *WKCS*, Wednesday, June 6, 1934, p. 8.

50. "A Harvest of Quilting," *KCS*, Wednesday, October 28, 1931, p. 24; and "A Quilt Exhibit Friday," *KCS*, Monday, June 15, 1931, p. 8.

51. "Quilters in Southwest Kansas Have a Show Day," *WKCS*, Wednesday, June 10, 1931, p. 7.

52. "Told History of Quilts," *KCS*, Wednesday, March 14, 1934, p. 18.

53. "Exhibit of 300 Quilts," *KCS*, Tuesday, February 2, 1932, p. 22, and "Old and New Quilts Vie for Awards in Exhibition," *KCS*, Wednesday, February 3, 1932, p. 12.

54. *KCS*, Wednesday, October 7, 1931, p. 7. In a news article in the same paper ("731 Quilts on Display," p. 16), a larger number of quilts were mentioned as being on display, and a list of some of the early entrants suggested the widespread interest in quiltmaking, since their addresses were sometimes in towns 20 to 30 miles from Kansas City, and all but fifty of the quilts had been made within the previous two or three years.

Crazy Quilts and Outline Quilts: Popular Responses to the Decorative Art/ Art Needlework Movement, 1876–1893

Virginia Gunn

In the decade following the 1876 Centennial Exhibition in Philadelphia, what came to be known as a "decorative art craze" swept across America.[1] This craze would have a profound effect on decorating and quiltmaking in the Gilded Age between 1876 and 1893. Americans believed that the Centennial had stimulated this development of art and that no areas had "profited by it more than those connected with the furnishing and decoration of the home."[2]

Women were encouraged to experiment with new aesthetic styles and ideas in decorating. Eastlake or Queen Anne furniture became the fashionable replacement for the Victorian rosewood and walnut rococo styles which had reigned supreme for over thirty years. Art needlework embroidery began to replace the old-fashioned Berlin canvas work. Entrepreneurs and tradesmen encouraged the new aesthetic trends in furnishing and adorning homes, sensing that they would enjoy "commercial advantages."[3]

This interest in artistic homes was part of the Aesthetic Movement originating in England in the 1860s under the leadership of thinkers and artists such as John Ruskin and William Morris. The household art phase of this movement stressed that the home was "the foundation of all that is good" and that whatever made the home "more attractive, more beautiful, more useful" was worthy of "the attention and thought of the noblest and best of men and women."[4] A beautiful home would lift the morality and productivity of the people living in it.

While experts noted that "the tendency of art is towards cost and luxury," they also stressed that "in furnishing the home ... every

Virginia Gunn: 819 Quinby Ave, Wooster, OH 44691

man or woman, rich or poor, should find a field for the display of individual taste."[5] To aid this process, many felt that the country needed "an institution that would establish a standard of taste which would preclude the possibility of the acceptance, with any degree of toleration, of such enormities as are now thrust upon the public."[6]

The Philadelphia Centennial would provide the stimulus for the formation of such taste-setting institutions. Within two years of this exhibition, a growing number of art schools, decorative art societies and women's exchanges were established in cities and towns across the country. New journals such as *The Art Journal, The Art Amateur* and *The Art Interchange* began serving those interested in household and decorative art. *The Art Amateur* summarized the trend:

> Art societies have sprung up all over the country. It is the fashion to talk about art and, in a fashionable way, to prac-tise it. Young ladies, instead of spending their mornings at the piano ... take lessons in painting on china, in oils, or water-colors, or ply their nimble fingers in the production of "art needle work."[7] (See Figure 1)

This paper will explore the role of the Decorative Art Societies, Societies of Art Needlework, or Women's Exchanges, in shaping the form of quiltmaking from 1876–1893. Proliferating after the Centennial Exhibition, they became taste setters during the household art phase of America's Aesthetic Movement. By promoting new types of embroidered bed coverings and rejecting calico patchwork as artistic needlework, these organizations influenced women's quilt-making decisions. Women wishing to participate in the art move-ment and to continue making quilts required new forms of ex-pression. Crazy quilts and outline quilts emerged as grass-roots responses to Aesthetic Movement fashions.

In the 1860s and early 1870s sophisticated people no longer chose traditional calico quilts or woven coverlets for their beds. These were replaced or covered with white Marseille spreads and other commercial spreads. According to one contemporary needlework expert, patchwork now fell "more under the head of plain than fancy needlework." Calico squares were useful for teaching little girls to sew or for old women who no longer being able to "conquer the intricacies of fine work, will still make patchwork quilts for coming generations." While some beautiful specimens were occasionally

Fig. 1. This illustration, part of a series, appeared in Demorest's Monthly Magazine *(September 1879), p. 504. A young lady is standing in a room which reflects the decorative art trends in home furnishing.*

seen at fancy fairs or county fairs, "the taste is one that has nearly died out."[8]

The reviewer who covered the Centennial Exhibition for *Arthur's Magazine* was not taken with American patchwork. She grouped it in the same category with the "abomination of worsted embroidery ... horrible to behold" and reported that "we saw some little patch-work, though not an abundance of it, we are happy to state."[9]

In Frank Leslie's *Historical Register of the Centennial Exposition* only one American quilt was described. This so-called quilt, sent by a woman from Alabama, was not the traditional type. It had a white satin background on which were "embroidered 1,500 roses and rosesbuds, in each of which there are from 500 to 900 stitches. Seven thousand skeins of silk were used in this work, and a lady was engaged upon it eighteen months."[10] Obviously there was still an interest in demanding decorative work.

Many reviews of the Centennial Exhibition paid particular attention to the Japanese display which was the most extensive ever shown in the Western world. Visitors were treated to the "full flower and glory of Japanese Art" and could admire wonderful bronzes, embroideries, costumes, silk textiles and decorative screens. One author felt that the Japanese and Chinese displays were "more artistic, beautiful, and attractive than those of any other nation" and predicted that they would "exert a wide and positive influence upon American art industries." He also forecast that this influence would not take the form of direct copying but would instead be expressed in design attempts to capture the "originality and poetic feeling which give to Japanese art its distinctive character."[11]

The exhibit of The Royal School of Art Needlework from Kensington, England was also popular. This school was established in 1872 for the two-fold purpose of restoring "ornamental needlework to the high place it once held among decorative arts" while at the same time supplying "suitable employment for poor gentlewomen."[12] Needy gentlewomen completed a three year training program in art needlework. They were then paid to execute designs copied from antique sources or drawn by leading aesthetic designers like William Morris, Walter Crane and Fairfax Wade. The ladies worked in anonymous privacy at the school's workrooms and their embroidered articles were sold in a salesroom maintained by the school.

The Royal School's art needlework display at the Centennial included embroidered bedspreads with patterns based on medieval or Rennaissance designs or conventionalized treatment of botanical subjects. While taste setters would later remember that beautifully embroidered quilts "formed the most practical feature of the display of decorative art-needlework," immediate reactions to these new embroideries were mixed.[13] *Peterson's Magazine* admired the harmonious effect of Fairfax Wade's arabesque design but felt the spread was marred by the insertion of coarse lace. *Arthur's Magazine* described a number of the bedspreads but felt that "beyond richness of material, brilliancy of coloring and elaborateness of design, there is little to recommend those things."[14] It appears that admiration of this new work was something that had to be learned over time.

However, the Royal School's idea of doing needlework for gainful employment was appealing. The Civil War and the early 1870s depression had thrown an increasing number of middle class wives into the category of "reduced ladies" who needed to earn their own living or supplement their husbands' meager wages. Women were looking for new ways to earn money respectably. Opportunities for women's employment were quite limited, especially for women not educated to teach. Domestic work, sales work or factory work held little appeal to middle-class women.

One of the visitors to the Royal School's display was Mrs. Candace Wheeler, a woman who moved in the art circles of New York City. Aware of friends who needed to discreetly supplement their incomes, she was happy to find that the new art needlework did not look too complicated. Skilled at needlework herself, she felt the designs and techniques involved were simple enough to make a similar project feasible in America.[15]

After returning to New York City and testing the idea with friends, Mrs. Wheeler worked to establish a similar institution. The New York Society of Decorative Arts was formed in the spring of 1877. New York socialite Mrs. David Lane was asked to be president. She formed a board of directors composed of the social and intellectual elite of the city. With the backing of the wealthy and influential, the Society was assured of receiving favorable publicity for its activities and displays.

The Society began to offer classes in decorative art techniques. A teacher, Mrs. Pode, was imported from England to direct the classes in art needlework. In October 1877, the Society "opened a salesroom at No. 4 East Twentieth Street, for sculpture, paintings, woodcarvings, lacework, needlework, tapestries, hangings, and other decorative works, selected from contributions sent chiefly by women from all parts of the country."[16] (See Figure 2) While hoping to help needy gentlewomen, the Society made "no distinctions as to the class of contributors" and was thus organized in a more democratic fashion than its English counterpart.[17]

So successful was the project that during its first three months the Society sold almost five thousand dollars worth of goods. *The Art Journal* noted that the society had "received the sympathy and support of the intelligent public," who had "made its decisions authorities in matters of decorative art."[18]

Within a year the Society had "flourishing branches in every

Fig. 2. This plate, originally published in Scribner's Monthly (September 1881), p. 698, gives a glimpse of the salesroom of The Society of Decorative Art in New York City.

State from Maine to Florida, and valuable auxiliaries in seventeen different cities," including Boston, Philadelphia, Charleston, Baltimore, Chicago, St. Louis and Detroit.[19] Called by a variety of names, these schools of art needlework or decorative art societies spread the ideals, values and tastes of the original group from coast to coast. (See Figure 3) The cause was also helped when the New York Society began its own publication, The Art Interchange, on September 18, 1878. This publication was to be "devoted to the subject of art as applied to household adornment" and gave "instruction, in silk, crewel, tapestry, and medieval embroideries ... and full descriptions of all novel fancy work."[20] Books such as Women's Handiwork in Modern Homes by Constance Carey Harrison (New

SCHOOL FOR EMBROIDERY, BOSTON ART MUSEUM.

Fig. 3. This plate which originally appeared in Harper's New Monthly Magazine *(May 1879), p. 839, shows the work room of the School of Needlework at the Boston Art Museum. It later united with* The Boston Society of Decorative Art.

York: Scribners, 1881), used the Society as the source for many ideas and helped spread its influence.

The New York Society of Decorative Art remained the pacesetter for taste nationally, although other schools and societies had wide influence as well. *Scribner's Monthly Magazine* did caution that "probably in many cases the stream grows shallow as it gets away from the source, and the quality of work approved by the Society deteriorates, to the disadvantage of the latter's reputation."[21]

As knowledge of the Society spread, more and more women sent contributions of handiwork to be sold. Since most contributors were untrained amateurs, the Society established a screening committee to accept or reject proffered items. Offerings which met the highest standards of excellence in form, color and workmanship

could be granted the Society's seal of merit. If articles were unaccept-
able, they were returned accompanied by a note from the secretary
offering helpful suggestions. *The Art Amateur* stated that "a good
standard of excellence in work has been maintained by a committee
who set their faces as flint against artistic rubbish."[22] Certain
categories of mechanical work were not considered artistic, and
"leather-work, knitting, Berlin wool-work, skeletonised leaves, and
much of the same class, are on this ground invariably excluded."[23]
The Society urged people to visit their salesrooms. There was no
better way for workers to learn "the right direction for their efforts,
than by seeing work which has passed the ordeal of a discriminating
judgement, and been found worthy of acceptance."[24]

Mrs. Candace Wheeler, a member of the screening committee, began to feel rather early that philanthropy and art might not mix
well. She knew that many well-made, useful items worthy of being
sold had to be rejected by the Society because they did not meet
artistic standards. Feeling that a new type of market was needed, she
left the Society to help Mrs. William Choate found the Women's
Exchange in the summer of 1878. The Women's Exchange had a
more liberal acceptance policy and its salesroom featured domestic
work such as bread, cakes, jams and pickles, as well as decorative art
work and needlework in "every form of plain and fancy sewing."[25]

The Exchange idea was very successful. In the first year the New
York Women's Exchange paid out $10,252 to consignees. Exchanges
were soon started in other cities. By 1892, seventy-five of the more
than one hundred exchanges which were established were still flourishing in twenty-three states.[26]

Demorest's Magazine felt that "to those interested in women's work
as a study, learning what she would do if she could, the rooms of the
Exchange are more interesting than those of the older society, for
this organization having a charitable basis a greater variety of work
is accepted."[27] With this in mind, it is interesting to reflect on Lucy
Salmon's comments when she wrote about the Exchanges for *Forum*
magazine in 1892. She stated that the Exchange "has raised the
standard of decorative and artistic needle-work by incorporating
into its rules a refusal to accept calico patchwork, wax, leather, hair,
feather, rice, spatter, splinter, and cardboard work."[28] This clearly
indicates that calico patchwork was placed in a class with other un-
fashionable decorative arts, even by the institution that had less
stringent artistic standards than the Decorative Art Societies.

Rejection of patchwork is seldom this explicit in articles published during the 1880s. This is understandable, for such a stand would have offended many rural subscribers. But such judgments can often be inferred from other remarks. In addition, traditional patchwork is never mentioned in descriptions of items on display in the salesrooms of either the Society or the Women's Exchange. This reinforces the supposition that there was a ban of sorts on calico patchwork in some of the institutions. Writing in 1921, Candace Wheeler recalled that after the middle of the nineteenth century, most patchwork was "a farmhouse industry" with "narrow limits," although in the "mountains of Kentucky and North Carolina, it still survives in its original painstaking excellence."[29]

It was clear that traditional patchwork quilts were not valued by taste setting institutions of the new Art Needlework and Decorative Art Movements. Therefore, if quiltmakers wanted to incorporate these fashionable trends into their work, they would have to adapt their familiar forms in some way. The new Art Needlework movement put heavy emphasis on surface embroidery instead of counted work which they considered to be mechanical and repetitious. Ideally, the new artistic needleworker would proceed in this way:

> The embroiderer designs her own pattern, and draws it
> directly on the material, shading and coloring according to
> her own fancy, so that every effective piece of crewel em-
> broidery may be considered a work of art.[30]

The needle artist was to paint with threads as an artist painted with a brush. Some women preferred painting on fabric to embroidery, and articles on silk painting appeared in magazines along with embroidery advice.[31] Americans who embroidered soon developed a preference for working in silk thread on silk or plush fabrics instead of embroidering on crash with crewel yarns as was more common in England. They also preferred natural and realistic designs to the conventionalized English ones and liked exotic designs from foreign cultures like Japan.

While ideal art work would be totally original, most publications believed it was acceptable to use designs furnished by trained designers, since becoming proficient at design was held to be a matter of years of study. The Decorative Art Society encouraged originality, but "if a thing be true it need not be original, the intention of the society being to encourage Art-work, and not merely to preside over the development of genius."[32] In fact, it was far better to use a good design by someone else than a poor one of your own.

In January 1881, *Harper's Bazar* announced that they were the first to have the privilege of publishing designs from the Kensington Royal School of Art Needlework, a feat they considered "proof of rare journalistic enterprise." They also published designs from the Decorative Art Society, and stated they were happy to cooperate with both groups in "their praiseworthy endeavors to disseminate and popularize a knowledge of the true principles of household art, and thus to beautify the homes of the people."[33] The Royal School's designs bore a distinctive logo which distinguished their authentic designs from attempted copies.

The designs were given in black and white outline form, with no indication of how they were to be shaded and only meager color suggestions, if any. Making a wise selection and placement of colors was felt to be difficult. Many women preferred to merely outline the design using a well known stem or outline stitch which came to be called the Kensington Stitch for outline embroidery. The J.F. Ingalls Company stated, "If embroidery is new to you, the outline work is best to commence on, as it is much easier to make than the Kensington embroidery, and requires no shading."[34] Women realized that "for outline-work many designs will be found simple and easy to work which would be quite impossible in crewels."[35] (See Figure 4.)

Even the taste setters found well designed outline work acceptable for bed quilts or coverlets. The New York Society of Decorative Art had a special category for outline work on silk at the 1881 exhibition. The prize-winning design for an outlined baby blanket was published in *Harper's Bazar*. *Arthur's Magazine* suggested copying Kate Greenaway figures from nursery books to make an outline quilt.[36]

Most art publications and women's magazines used the term quilt very loosely. The directions usually indicate that they are suggesting a lined or hemmed bed covering when they write of quilts. *The Art Amateur* recognized this and explained:

> A quilt means, properly speaking, something quilted—i.e. wadded and sewn down ... In these days, and with a decorative end in view, such very elaborate work hardly repays the time spent on it; but the coverlet is to be recommended as an excellent object for work and for design. Outline work

Fig. 4. *These outline designs were given in* The Ladies' Manual of Fancy
Work *published by A.L. Burt of New York in 1884. Kate Greenaway type
figures and floral patterns were often used on quilt blocks for outline quilts.*

    in one color is very suitable for this purpose, and a bold
    formal pattern looks very handsome.[37]
While the taste setters generally had an embroidered spread in
mind, many women familiar with traditional patchwork techniques
preferred to combine their outline embroidery with "proper quilting." It was easy for them to embroider outline patterns on familiar
blocks, set them together and quilt them in the traditional way. The
majority of these "outline quilts" were made for children and were
meant to be used and washed. Therefore women usually outlined
with Turkey red or blue cotton embroidery floss, the most colorfast
yarns.

    Publications offered outline designs from the leading schools and
societies, as well as from other sources. Needy artists found creating
such designs a good way to raise money. Since there were no copy-
right laws, designs from the most prestigious sources were frequently
pirated and copied. Eventually, opportunistic entrepreneurs flooded
the market with inexpensive designs. Companies such as J.F. Ingalls
and T.E. Parker of Lynn, Massachusetts, advertised pattern cata-
logues in the backs of women's magazines. The taste setters warned
that many of "the patterns commonly sold in the stores are utterly
valueless."[38] Mrs. Julian Hawthorne informed readers of *Harper's
Bazar* that designs from "nursery tales illustrated by badly drawn,
oddly dressed children ... may be fashionable, but they are not

necessarily artistic."[39] In spite of this criticism, outline embroidery became popular because it was "very effective, very rapidly done, and very cheap."[40]

These "outline quilts" allowed quiltmakers to continue their traditional skills while incorporating new fashions in outline and art needlework. However, these practical, washable quilts did not satisfy all needs to create something ornamental, decorative and individual. Quilters were familiar with the fancy silk fabrics and embroidery used on portieres and screens in the homes of the fashionable elite. Women's periodicals and art journals often described magnificent home furnishings made for the wealthy. They believed, as did *Harper's Bazar*, that the "rare and beautiful things ... furnishing the grand drawing-rooms of millionaires ... are of interest ... mainly because they set the fashions for the simpler things used by people of small means."[41] Quiltmakers must have found the crazy quilt a perfect solution for imitating the fashionable trends and incorporating them into the quiltmaking process.

The exact origin of the crazy quilt was discussed in the periodicals of the early 1880s. Many were willing to hazard a guess, but no one was certain—though most would probably have agreed with *Demorest's*, that the crazy quilt "came in with what is rudely denominated the "decorative craze."[42] It is likely that crazy quilts were a grass roots response to the decorative art movement.

The first descriptions of this new type of needlework appearing in popular women's magazines were rather vague, and the technique remained unnamed. For example, in November 1879, *Peterson's Magazine*, describing table covers, reported a "new work, which consists of scraps of all kinds being appliqued on to serge, and ornamented with colored silks, in imitation of Eastern work."[43] Janett Rets, writing for *Demorest's*, states that "the old patchwork quilts, which usurped so large a portion of our grandmother's time, are replaced by others made in more elaborate style, which, if well done, are quite Eastern in effect ... These quilts are quite bewildering in their combination of colors and stuffs."[44] *Harper's Bazar* said that "we have quite discarded in our modern quilts the regular geometric design once so popular, and substituted what are more like the changing figures of the kaleidoscope, or the beauty and infinite variety of Oriental mosaics."[45]

The fact that these descriptions appeared first in the editorial columns rather than in the work table sections of the magazines suggests that crazy quilts were observed rather than introduced by these periodicals. Editors recognized oriental influence. Several of them felt this new work was related to mid-Victorian silk template quilts often called mosaic patchwork. However, crazy quilts were not made by cutting irregular templates. Instead, the technique used on the well-known log cabin quilts was adapted. Traditional quilt-makers were very familiar with the pressed patchwork method of fashioning log cabin quilts by adding strips of wool, cotton or silk to a foundation or background fabric. It would be easy to understand how an assymetrical arrangement of silk strips around an irregular center might be considered a Japanese effect. If combined with embroidery and art needlework designs, all the fashionable decorating trends could be incorporated in one unique grass roots interpretation. Hetta Ward supported this theory of development when she wrote:

> Careful housewives have always hoarded their bright bits of silk and old ribbons, and years ago, these were fashioned with painful regularity and great labor into what were called log-cabin bed-spreads ... Of late years these same bits of bright silk have been again used for bed-spreads, but put together in a happy hit-or-miss fashion, joined with a slight line of embroidery and called Japanese bed-spreads.[46]

The Decorative Art Societies probably did not introduce crazy work in their workrooms since these were under the direction of an English needleworker and favored the type of conventional embroidery produced in England. It is likely that crazy quilts were first introduced to the Societies by some contributor to the salesrooms rather than by an instructor. At any rate, the taste setters recognized the work and felt that if it was properly done it offered "an opportunity for really artistic work." In October 1882, *The Art Amateur* presented its first article on "crazy" quilts. The editor noted that:

> When the present favorite style of quilt was introduced it was called the Japanese, but the national sense of humor has been too keen, and the Japanese is now generally known as the "crazy" quilt. There is method in its madness, however, and put together with a good understanding of color effects, the crazy quilt may prove an artistic piece of work.[47]

The description of the technique given in this article reveals that

y quilts were fully developed by 1882. The article states:

The foundation of the crazy quilt consists of patches of calico, or any other humble material ten inches square. On each of these squares is laid a large irregular piece of silk, the largest used in the square, which is called the "starter." It is usually placed at some angle covering the centre, and it is advisable that this piece be of some light, plain color. The rest of the square is then filled up with odd pieces of silk which are simply overlapped and basted down, with the raw edges turned in... The overlapping seams are covered with fancy stitches in silk and filoselle, arrasene or gold thread. The herring-bone is the simplest form of stitch used, but it is generally employed in combinations of color and with the addition of point Russe, cross-stitch, feather stitch, and every sort in fact which the ingenious fingers of women can devise. It is impossible to give directions in this respect; the individual fancy should have free play and nothing will come amiss. These stitches are not confined to the seams, but are used at discretion in the body of the pieces, or wherever the needle-woman's fancy may direct. Applique work is also sometimes employed on the pieces. Sunflowers and daisies in other stuffs, such as velvet and plush, may be introduced, together with Greek vases, Japanese teapots, and Etruscan jars. This is done, however, with doubtful taste.[48]

The author of this article suggests that on "this last and supremest development of the crazy quilt ... the results are often handsome enough to warrant the enthusiasm and industry expended in producing them." There is a warning, however, against cluttering the surface with odd things that would look good on close inspection but would add nothing to the general effect.[49] This comment indicates an awareness that crazy quilts were made to be admired and inspected, often at close range. Women made these quilts to be shown off as works of art. It was felt that the piece-de-resistance of crazy work was the bedspread, and *Harper's Bazar* wrote that such a work "deserves to be handed down to posterity as an heirloom."[50] The size of the crazy quilt is usually smaller than traditional bed coverings, for "these quilts, even when used on a bed are not tucked in like ordinary ones."[51] *Godey's Lady's Book* stated that "ornamental coverlets are rarely made full size ... [they] lay on top of the bed after it is made, over the ordinary white quilt."[52] This manner of use allowed them to be seen and admired.

While crazy quilts were usually artistic masterpieces for the makers' own homes, some were also made for sale. *Demorest's* reported that "these quilts are seen occasionally in shop windows marked with fabulous prices."[53] They reportedly sold at seventy-five to a hundred dollars. One, with Oscar Wilde and sunflowers, sold at a fair for $150.00.[54] However, since crazy quilts took much time and material to make, the technique was often used on smaller items such as sofa-pillows, chair-tidies, table-covers and decorative scarfs. These sold well at the Women's Exchanges.[55]

With crazy work recognized at the highest levels in needlework circles, crazy work became a "mania for home decoration" by 1883.[56] *Dorcas Magazine* wrote that:

> Of all the "crazes" which have swept over and fairly engulfed some of us, there is none which has taken a deeper hold upon the fair women of our land than this one of crazy patchwork ... Many a women with strong artistic taste finds no other outlet for it than in such work as this.[57]

The Art Amateur reported that:

> One of the ambitions of a young man of fashion nowadays is the possession of a crazy quilt, made up of patches contributed by the ladies of his acquaintance; and his social progress may be reckoned by these patches as an Indian warrior's prowess is reckoned by his scalps.[58] (See Figure 5)

The crazy quilt enthusiasm was fanned by entrepreneurs providing materials, designs and directions in a seemingly mad rush to capitalize and extract a profit from this "decorative craze." In the April 1884 issue of *The Ladies Home Journal*, seven different companies ran ads for patchwork silks on one page.[59] Penny McMorris's beautiful book *Crazy Quilts* clearly documents the crazy quilt at the peak of its popularity in the mid 1880s. One can see the amazing and rich variety of individual interpretations in this technique.[60]

As crazy work became popular and widespread, it lost much of its appeal among the taste setters. Editors of *Dorcas* discussing crazy quilts in 1884 noted that "many a country girl finds her only relief from an uncongenial life and unpleasant duties in the fancy work which the 'high art' people delight to condemn."[61] The same year an editor of *Harper's Bazar* began to write that "the craze for decorative

Fig. 5. This cabinet photograph taken in 1880s is a good example of the aesthetic influence on interior back-grounds in the studio. The crazy-work scarf is prominently displayed and helps suggest that this is a "young man of fashion." (author's collection)

art has wrought certain definite mischiefs with much good ... the makers of Kensington-stitch table-cloth borders, Holbein towel ends, 'decorative waste-baskets' ... and 'crazy patchwork' seem to have eaten of the insane root that takes reason prisoner. Their countless stitches and ugly ingenuity appear to them the fit expression of aesthetic instincts."[62] In spite of these opinions, crazy quilts flourished. By 1887, *Godey's Lady's Book* found that "the time, patience, stitches and mistakes the crazy quilt represents, are too awful for words." Reporting on the Second Competitive Exhibition of Needlework sponsored by the Canfield Company and held in New York City in December 1887, *Godey's* stated that "we regretted much the time and energy spent on the most childish, and unsatisfactory of all work done with the needle, 'crazy' patch-work, and we strongly recommend that prizes for such work be omitted from all future announcements."[63]

Interviewed in 1887, Mrs. Candace Wheeler, now running "The Associated Artists," her own design firm, opined that "there is far too much embroidery, too much so-called 'ornamentation' in our houses ..." She wished she "could turn all the miserable waste of embroidery into legitimate channels" and decried "the wretched fashion journals that have flooded the country with discordant designs, made by cheap designers, regardless of or in ignorance of the laws of color and composition."[64]

Crazy quilts continued to be made in abundance well into the twentieth century, although they eventually ceased to be featured in leading periodicals. Later versions were often less ornate and detailed in design. It was noted that modern women were in a hurry, and had "neither the time, skill, nor patience for the finer and more elaborate kinds of art embroidery."[65] Outline quilts remained popular for children. The design motifs changed to reflect trends in story books. Peter Rabbit and the Sunbonnet babies replaced the Kate Greenaways and Brownies of the 19th century. In the 1890s, interest in traditional calico patchwork, long out of favor, began to re-emerge.[66]

The era of the crazy quilt and Kensington outline work gradually became part of history, and interest in the decorative art, art needlework and household arts movements subsided. Many of the decorative art journals ceased publication. Most decorative art societies gradually faded from the scene in the late 19th and early 20th centuries as people became convinced once again that art should be in the hands of trained experts instead of amateurs. The Women's Exchanges lasted through the depression, and some still exist today. For the most part, however, the art world turned its back on needlework, which was once again seen mainly as a pastime for women in the home.

Modern scientific efficiency became the trend of the early 20th century. This movement favored a clean, uncluttered home where the decorative crazy quilt would look out of place. Many of them were packed away and saved, for they were scrapbooks of memories—reminders of an age when women followed the household art aesthetic trends by making "artistic quilts" to decorate their homes. Margaret E. Sangster captures the mood and meaning of this unique time in her poem, "The Crazy Quilt," published in 1884:

THE CRAZY QUILT
By Margaret E. Sangster.

Patchwork only, did you say,
This mosaic quaint and gay,
Starred with dainty applique,
    In confusion mazy?
Sooth it hath a high-born air,
With an easeful charm and rare,
Lightening the weight of care.
    Wherefore call it crazy?

Every woman in the land
This bewitching quilt has planned;
Slender fingers, toil-worn hand,
    Pulse alike with pleasure
As the curious pieces blend
This an heirloom's grace to lend,
That the souvenir of a friend,
    Each a cherished treasure.

Patiently dear grandma sets
Bit to bit, and swift forgets
All the little daily frets
    Age and loss are bringing,
And we hear her softly croon
To herself a tender tune;
'Tis of youth and love a rune
    She is gently singing.

Shaking heads and looking wise,
Merchants smile with doubtful eyes
When, expectant of a prize,
    Maidens beg a sample.

Stock of velvet, silk, or frieze,
Like the famous nibbled cheese,
Disappears if, dames to please,
   Clipped are fragments ample.

Patchwork 'tis, but glorified,
Aureoled with stately pride,
Fit to offer to a bride
   As a wedding present.
Stitched with more than common pains,
Offspring of artistic brains,
Wrought in flowers, and loops, and chains,
   Is this patchwork pleasant.[67]

Notes and References:

1. "Is Our Art Only a Fashion?" *The Art Amateur*, (June 1881), p. 2.
2. "Hints for Home Furnishing," *The Art Amateur*, (July 1879), p. 34.
3. "Is Our Art Only a Fashion?" p. 2.
4. Charles W. Elliot, "Household Art," *The Art Journal* (New York: Appleton, 1875), p. 295. For further information on the Aesthetic Movement and the Household Art Movement, see Elizabeth Aslin, *The Aesthetic Movement: Prelude to Art Nouveau* (N.Y.: Praeger, 1969); Martha Crabill McClaugherty, "Household Art: Creating the Artistic Home, 1868–1893," *Winterthur Portfolio* (Spring 1983), pp. 1–26; and Gwendolyn Wright, *Moralism & the Model Home* (University of Chicago Press, 1980).
5. Elliot, p. 295; "Hints for Home Furnishing," p. 34.
6. "American Art," *Demorest's Monthly Magazine*, (November 1875). p. 458.
7. "Is Our Art Only a Fashion?" p. 2.

8. S. Annie Frost, *The Ladies Guide to Needlework and Embroidery* (New York: Henry T. Williams, 1877), p. 128.

9. E.B.D., "The Great Centennial Exhibition," *Arthur's Illustrated Home Magazine*, (August 1876), p. 453.

10. *Historical Register of the Centennial Exposition*, (New York: Frank Leslie, 1876), p. 156.

11. George Ward Nichols, *Art Education Applied to Industry* (New York: Harper and Brothers, 1877), p. 181, 176–177.

12. "The Royal School of Art-Needlework, South Kensington," *The Art Journal* (1875), p. 300; Mrs. Julian Hawthorne, "South Kensington Royal School of Art Needle-Work," *Harper's Bazar*, (January 15, 1881), p. 38.

13. "Patchwork," *Harper's Bazar*, (September 16, 1882), p. 583.

14. "Editor's Table," *Peterson's Magazine*, (August 1876), p. 150; "The Great Centennial Exhibition," *Arthur's Magazine*, (August 1876), p. 451.

15. Candace Wheeler, *Yesterdays in a Busy Life* (New York: Harper & Bros., 1918), pp. 209–12. See also Madeline B. Stern, *We the Women* (New York: Schulte Publishing Co., 1963), Chapter 12, "An American Woman First in Textiles and Interior Decoration — Candace Wheeler," pp. 273–303.

16. "Introductory — The Society of Decorative Art in the City of New York," *The Art Journal* (1878), pp. 173–79.

17. Arthur B. Turnure, "The Society of Decorative Art," *The Art Journal* (1870), p. 50.

18. "Introductory — The Society of Decorative Art...", pp. 174–175.

19. Turnure, p. 56; "The Decorative Art Society's Rooms," *The Art Amateur* (July 1879), p. 47.

20. "The Art Interchange," *Arthur's Illustrated Home Magazine*, (December 1878), p. 605; "The Art Interchange," *The Art Journal*, (1878), p. 320.

21. "The Society of Decorative Art (New York)," *Scribner's Monthly Magazine* (September 1881), p. 703.

22. Calista Halsey, "The Decorative Art Society Rooms," *The Art Amateur* (June 1879), p. 10.

23. Turnure, p. 53.

24. "Modes and Methods of Work," *The Art Interchange*, (September 18, 1878), p. 1.

25. Lucy M. Salmon, "The Woman's Exchange: Charity or Business?" *The Forum*, (May 1892), p. 395; Candace Wheeler, *Yesterdays in a Busy Life*, pp. 224–9.

26. Ellen E. Dickinson, "New York Exchange for Women's Work," *The Art Amateur*, (July 1879), p. 35; Lucy M. Salmon, p. 396.

27. G.R., "Decorative Art Work By Women—Notes Collected In New York Art Rooms," *Demorest's Monthly Magazine*, (July 1885), p. 584.

28. Lucy M. Salmon, p. 402.

29. Candace Wheeler, *The Development of Embroidery in America* (New York: Harper and Bros, 1921), pp. 58–60.

30. "Art Embroidery," *Arthur's Illustrated Home Magazine*, (November 1878), p. 550.

31. "Silk Painting," *Harper's Bazar*, (August 26, 1882), p. 539. See also "Art Embroidery," *Godey's Lady's Book*, (October 1884), p. 418.

32. Turnure, pp. 52–53; L. Higgin, "The Art of Embroidery—Concerning Design," *The Art Amateur*, (November 1886), p. 130.

33. "Needle-Work Designs From South Kensington," *Harper's Bazar*, (January 1, 1881), p. 2.

34. *Ingall's Manual of Fancy Work, New (1884) Edition* (Lynn, Mass.: J.F. Ingalls, 1882), unnumbered p. 40.

35. "Outline Embroidery," *Harper's Bazar*, (November 2, 1878), p. 699. See also Mrs. Julian Hawthorne, "Crewel-Work," *Harper's Bazar*, (March 18, 1882), p. 167.

36. "Prize Design for Baby Blanket—Outline Work," *Harper's Bazar*, (August 26, 1882), pp. 541–542; "Kate Greenaway Quilt," *Arthur's Home Magazine*, (November 1882), p. 696.

37. "Objects for Needlework Decoration," *The Art Amateur*, (September 1879), p. 86.

38. Charles Barnard, "The New Embroidery," *Demorest's Monthly Magazine*, (April 1884), p. 365.

39. Mrs. Julian Hawthorne, "True Art-Needle-Work," *Harper's Bazar*, (October 29, 1881), p. 694.

40. Mrs. Jane Weaver, "Designs For D'oylies," *Peterson's Magazine*, (December 1880), p. 462.

41. "New York Fashions: House-Furnishing," *Harper's Bazar*, (May 27, 1882), p. 323.

42. Lisle Lester, "Crazy Patchwork," *Demorest's Monthly Magazine*, (August 1884), p. 619.

43. "Editor's Table—Making Table Borders." *Peterson's Magazine*, (November 1879),p. 406; See also Ella R. Church, *Artistic Embroidery* (New York: Adams & Bishop, 1880), p. 28, where a table-cover with this type of work is reported.

44. Janette R. Rets, "Finishing Touches," *Demorest's Monthly Magazine*, (November 1882), p. 27.

45. "Patchwork," *Harper's Bazar*, (September 16, 1882), p. 583. This article includes clear instructions for the technique, although it is not called crazy work.

46. Hetta L.H. Ward, "Home Art and Home Comfort—Bed-Spreads," *Demorest's Monthly Magazine*, (April 1884), p. 362.
47. " 'Crazy' Quilts," *The Art Amateur*, (October 1882), p. 108.
48. *Ibid.*
49. *Ibid.*
50. "Patchwork," *Harper's Bazar*, (September 16, 1882), p. 583.
51. "Crazy Patchwork," *Dorcas Magazine*, (October 1884), p.264.
52. "New Fancy Work," *Godey's Lady's Book*, (September 1887), p. 211.
53. Hetta L.H. Ward, p. 362; Lisle Lester, p. 622.
54. "Crazy Work" in *Treasures of Use and Beauty* (Springfield, Mass.: W.C. King and Co., 1883), p. 461. See also: "Mosaic Patchwork—Continued," *Godey's Lady's Book*, (May 1883), p. 463.
55. Mrs. M.L. Rayne, *What Can A Woman Do?* (Detroit, St. Louis & Cincinnati: F.B. Dickerson, 1885), p. 152.
56. *Treasures of Use and Beauty*, pp. 460–461.
57. "Crazy Patchwork," *Dorcas Magazine*, (October 1884), p. 263.
58. "Crazy Quilts," *The Art Amateur*, p. 108.
59. *The Ladies Home Journal* (April 1884), p. 5.
60. Penny McMorris, *Crazy Quilts* (New York: E.P. Dutton, 1984). See also Sally Garoutte's excellent pioneering article "The Development of Crazy Quilts," *Quilter's Journal*, (Fall 1978), pp. 13–15.
61. "Crazy Patchwork," *Dorcas Magazine*, (October 1884), p. 263.
62. "Crazy Work and Sane Work," *Harper's Bazar*, (September 13, 1884), p. 578.
63. "Instead of a Crazy Quilt," *Godey's Lady's Book*. (September 1887), p. 248; "The Second Competitive Exhibition of the Canfield Art Needlework," *Godey's Lady's Book*, (February 1888), pp. 182–185.
64. M.G.H. (Mary Gay Humphreys), "Embroidery in America—Mrs. Wheeler's Views," *The Art Amateur*, (January 1888), p. 46.
65. Emma Haywood, "Art Needlework—Hints on Embroidery," *The Art Amateur*, August 1890), p. 59.
66. See Cuesta Benberry, "The Twentieth Century's First Quilt Revival," *Quilter's Newsletter*, (July/August 1979), pp. 20–22 and Sybil Lanigan, "Revival of the Patchwork Quilt," *The Ladies' Home Journal*, (October 1894), p. 19.
67. Margaret E. Sangster, "The Crazy Quilt," *Harper's Bazar*, (January 12, 1884), p. 27.

Quilts in the WPA Milwaukee
Handicraft Project, 1935–1943

Merikay Waldvogel

In 1979 in Knoxville, Tennessee, I became intrigued with and subsequently bought a Sailboat quilt with some unusual source information stamped on the back. The rubber-stamped information
was smudged, but I could decipher "WPA Handicraft Project,
Milwaukee, Wisconsin, Sponsored by Milwaukee County and
Milwaukee State Teachers College." The project number was
unclear.

Having administered federal grants while directing a women's
employment project in Knoxville, in the late 1970s, I knew any fed-
erally funded project would have been required to submit numerous
reports on finances, staff, participants, products and program
design. So expecting there would be a wealth of documents, I began
my quilt research sending inquiries by mail to government sources.
Through the records at the Milwaukee County Historical Museum I
was able to determine that the number of the project was #8601.
From the National Archives I received a list of items sold, including
a reference to the Sailboat quilt. The Milwaukee County government notified me their records of the project had been destroyed
years before. The bulk of the information for this paper, however,
was discovered not in a government agency, but in the history section of the Milwaukee Public Museum.

That quilts serve as historical documents continues to be a de-
bated question. This search presents a strong case for the belief that
quilts do, in fact, serve as historical documents. Using information
on the quilt (the stamped insignia) and looking for answers to questions about unusual construction aspects of the quilt, I discovered
some of the history of a successful employment project which has

Merikay Waldvogel: 1501 Whitower Rd, Knoxville, TN 37919

faded from national attention. The purpose of the paper, therefore, is not only to share information on the quilts but also to share the history of the WPA Milwaukee Handicraft Project.

Background

The WPA Milwaukee Handicraft Project began in 1935 as an effort to employ all the women on the relief rolls in Milwaukee County. Up to that time the primary project for women in Milwaukee County was an industrial type sewing project making garments for inmates in the county's institutions. However, many women eligible for WPA employment lacked the skills and stamina to cope with the pressures of this type of machine work and there remained on the relief (welfare) rolls a large group of women seen as unskilled and therefore unfit to work.[1] Mrs. Harriet P. Clinton of the Women's Division of the WPA in Milwaukee County was determined to find a way to get women off relief. She approached Miss Elsa Ulbricht, an art professor at Milwaukee State Teachers College, to develop a project. Mrs. Clinton envisioned a project where unskilled women would compile scrapbooks to be used as coloring books and reading material for school age children. In fact, the scrapbooks *were* made, but Miss Ulbricht felt that

> it would be inexcusable ... to expend valuable time and effort to dissipate federal money on work which had no educational significance or did not contribute to the cultural development of the individual and the community.[2]

Therefore she developed a program that would give work to these unskilled women and would at the same time raise standards of crafts production. By selling the crafts to public institutions for the cost of the materials, she hoped also to give those people housed in the institutions a better understanding of fine handicrafts.

Miss Ulbricht, as the sponsor's agent, was responsible for hiring the staff. In outlining her requirements for staff she wrote:

> Experience in crafts and crafts materials, originality and a creative approach in solving problems (which meant at least two years' work in creative design and the crafts), college psychology applied to teaching situations and an interest and good understanding of people—these were qualifications met by imaginative, art trained individuals—generally four year art graduates.[3]

Fig. 1. Sailboat quilt. Author's collection.

Miss Ulbricht hired as staff members many of her own art students who themselves were without jobs when they graduated. Thus according to Mrs. Julia Loomis Knudson, a former staff member, the staff was very close-knit, very appreciative of the meaningful employment and very enthusiastic.[4]

On November 6, 1935 the Milwaukee Handicraft Project was ready to begin. Only one participant of an expected 250 showed up that first day because of a mixup in the notices, but by the end of

the second week 800 women were there. At first the women were
apprehensive. Miss Ulbricht described the participants during the
first days.

> They manifested uneasiness, uncertainty and great appre-
> hension of their ability to meet the needs of this job to
> which they had been indiscriminately assigned and of this
> project about which they knew nothing. Many of them
> had had no work or very meagre work experiences; many
> of them had been out of employment so many months that
> they had become disheartened and depressed. They were of
> all ages, all nationalities (some speaking very broken
> English), some could neither read nor write, Negro and
> white, of all degrees of intelligence and education. Many
> were poorly clothed, even unkempt, and some appeared
> physically weak from the lack of nourishment, medical at-
> tention and insecurity suffered for so long a time.[5]

But after a few weeks they were settled into a skill level at which
they could excel. They earned $50 per month and received some
medical attention.[6]

The project at its height was divided into four units: 1) book-
binding, 2) blockprinting, screenprinting, rug making, applique,
dollmaking, cloth toys and costumes, 3) weaving and 4) wood and
furniture.[7] Each unit produced items which were distributed at the
cost of materials only to tax-supported institutions. For example,
college dormitories were furnished with printed draperies, rugs and
furniture made by the project. Dolls were made for children in or-
phanages and the WPA nurseries. The staff often visited the institution before designing the products so that the particular location
and need were clear to them.

As word of the project's success spread, educators from around the
country toured the project classrooms and workshops in downtown
Milwaukee. Being impressed with the products they saw, the visitors
requested samples of the project's craft items to be used for educational purposes. The staff put together educational service kits
which were sold at cost of materials to school systems, libraries,
home economics colleges and museums all over the country. Port-
folios of block print samples are at the Art Institute of Chicago
Textile Department and at the Indianapolis Museum of Art. A set
of book bindings is in the history collection at the Milwaukee Public

Fig. 2. Cherry Tree quilt, 1938. 39.45, Indianapolis Museum of Art, Niblack Textile Fund. Photo: Robert Wallace.

Museum. Although the educational service kits were not originally planned, they were a source of unexpected orders for the project, and more importantly helped to fulfill one of the project's prime objectives: to raise the standards of crafts and crafts education.

The project was originally sponsored by the Milwaukee State Teachers College and was later taken over by the Milwaukee County government. After WPA funding ended, the County continued to operate a much-reduced project until the early 1970s. Over 5000 workers were assigned to the WPA-funded project during its eight-year existence between 1935 and 1943. The number of workers at any one time varied from 100 to 1350.[8]

There was much praise for the project. Alberta Redenbaugh who toured all the WPA crafts projects throughout the United States wrote:

> The handicraft unit at Milwaukee is perhaps the best known in the United States. Their organization is most efficient and their design is very good. Many of their products have commercial possibilities as they stand, especially their block printed hangings, their screen prints, toys and dolls. I

feel that the doll produced in this unit is the best I have seen anywhere and put in production should be saleable.[9]

Dr. Jane Betsey Welling, professor of education, Wayne State University, wrote in the February 1944 issue of *Design* devoted entirely to the Milwaukee Handicraft Project that

> I visited this project in the late thirties. There in a great room with temporary partitions made functionally gay by their own wares and material, I saw people of all ages, sizes, shapes, colors, nationalities, temperaments and cultures working together earnestly and with that sort of joy in work and pride in workmanship which comes only when there is true identification with one's work. Here was that creative spark which makes hard work play and products craftsman-like from start to finish. I had never seen the like before! I have not seen it since. Those competent workers whom I watched at work were a few months before the 'flotsam and jetsom' of an economic havoc which we were all feeling. They were the ones whom industry, education and society had discarded as useless and here they were before our very eyes creating quality products.[10]

The project's positive atmosphere was, however, sometimes countered by frustrations. Mrs. Mary June Kellogg Rice, the art director, pointed out that what they were doing was controversial. She said there was a bitter political tone in the country. The press was anti-WPA and anti-Roosevelt. Sometimes workers went home happy with their work only to hear their children's tales of being criticized for having a parent working for the WPA. Much of the country saw the WPA projects as make-work projects and thus a waste of tax-payers' money.[11]

Mrs. Rice also pointed out that the staff was terribly sensitive to the criticism that the WPA was competing with private industry.

> It was nonsense, of course, but we avoided words like "selling" and the idea that the project made a profit. WPA paid the workers, the County (as sponsor) provided the workshop space, the receiving institution paid the cost of materials. The Teachers College as co-sponsor, theoretically provided the services of Else Ulbricht, but she carried a full teaching load as well as giving so much of herself to the project.[12]

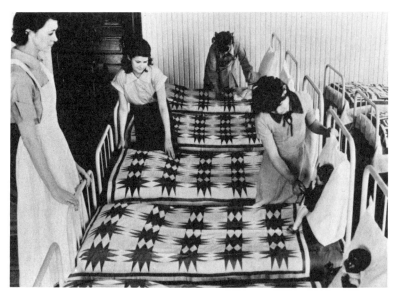

Fig. 3. Project quilts on orphanage children's beds. Photo courtesy Milwaukee County Public Museum.

Other frustrations included turnover of the workers. As people got other jobs, they left. New workers had to be trained. Maintaining the high standards which Miss Ulbricht strove for was difficult.

On the other hand, Mrs. Rice felt the successes resulted from the type and training of the staff members and the unusual combination of their design and supervision functions. The core of the staff was made up of enthusiastic, idealistic, energetic young people who were themselves grateful for jobs. It was a creative group sharing the same art background. "We knew each other, we knew Elsa Ulbricht; we reflected her philosophy about art, teaching and dealing with people."[13]

Mrs. Rice went on to point out that the positions of artist-foremen, which the staff held, meant that they not only designed the objects made by the workers under their supervision but also taught them the skills that were needed to produce these articles. The capabilities of each unskilled worker had to be evaluated and the work broken down into tasks each person could do. The staff's youthful enthusiasm, creative inventiveness and sympathy for society's cast-offs were very important ingredients in the success of the project.[14]

Miss Ulbricht's personality appears throughout the history of the project and probably was the most important reason for its success. She died in Milwaukee in 1980 at the age of 94. "The inventiveness of Ms. Ulbricht, a trained artist, made the project a success,"[15] writes Andy Leon Harney in "WPA Handicrafts Rediscovered" in *Historic Preservation* July-September 1973. "She always gave those who worked with her great freedom of expression which, she feels, is the only way to establish confidence and freedom to create with inspired effort to insure the best results,"[16] wrote Gertrude Copp. "Elsa was a remarkable woman and inspired teacher. A woman far ahead of her time,"[17] added Mrs. Rice, who was Elsa's student from elementary school days. "Elsa was a feminist of her time, very creative and very supportive of her students."[18] noted Grace Iacolucci, Ulbricht's student.

She was an eloquent fighter as evidenced in her own words in a letter to Mrs. Eleanor Roosevelt in 1941 pleading for continued funding for the project.

> In its broadest sense, this education became habilitation and rehabilitation. And as these unskilled people worked day by day, with joy in achievement and in a fundamental manner became conscious of their growth in appreciation as they gained skills,—without that fear which is often felt for "Object d'art"—men and women, young and old, white and black, side by side—there came tolerance for each other with freedom of deportment for participation in and responsibility for the task to be done,—a proved experiment that democratic procedure is RIGHT.[19]

Findings

The quilts made by the project had unusual features. The Sailboat quilt, for example, is an unusual size—40 by 60 inches—too large for a crib quilt and too small for a twin size bed.

The design of the quilt has a painterly quality to it; the central area is divided into fifteen blocks (seven by nine inches). Eight blocks of a sailboat with clean modern lines are alternately set beside seven plain blue blocks. The blocks are surrounded by six borders of varying widths and colors, much like a mat and frame. (See Figure 1.)

Fig. 4. Quilts on display at exhibit of the project. [1970] Photo courtesy Milwaukee County Public Museum.

The construction of the quilt is difficult to duplicate easily. First, the block's tiny irregularly shaped pieces with curved edges made it very difficult to piece. Second, the six borders created the problem of mitered corners, which even expert quilters avoid. Finally, the quilt has no batting, which may or may not be unusual for a quilt, but it posed a question as to the purpose for which it was made.

The quilting does not show as much inspiration as the block design; in fact, the quilting is very difficult to see because of the lack of batting. Quilting stitches follow the pieces of the block design; the sailboat outline, however, is quilted into the plain blue blocks.

Finally, the material used in the quilt is rather unusual for quilts made in the 1930s. Instead of gaily printed fabrics, pre-shrunk percale in solid colors only was used in the Sailboat quilt; eight different colors were used. There was obviously some expense in acquiring the fabric.

In an undated report entitled *WPA Handicraft Project 1170*, the first mention of quilts in the Milwaukee Handicraft Project was found.

> Making of quilts was not given a prominent place in the original set up of the project. When the project began to outfit two Milwaukee WPA nursery schools a place for quilts was found in a group which could legitimately benefit by WPA. The emergency nursery schools were well enough equipped in a way, but it was felt that the handicraft project could do much to add to the happiness of the underpriv-

ileged children who attended them by making them more
attractive and colorful. The dull gray comforters covered
the cots so it was decided to make patchwork quilts for each
cot. The gayest of colors have been used in these tiny quilts.
The state director of nursery schools was so pleased that
quilts were ordered for all the Wisconsin Emergency nursery schools, so a quilt department was organized employing
75 workers, one designer and three supervisors from the relief rolls. All quilts produced are original designs or adapta-
tions of very old patterns. Bright colors which appeal particularly to children are used throughout the quilts.[20]

Here are the answers to the size and construction questions; the
quilts were made to only cover the tops of the children's cots (thus
the small size) and, as the gray wool comforters provided warmth,
there was no need for batting.

Mrs. Julia Loomis Knudson, one of the quilt designers, cleared up
questions about the design. She said the quilts were designed by herself, Mrs. Dorothy Phillips Haagensen and several others; they were
particularly interested in developing whimsical designs which would
cheer up the children. None of the designers had had any experience with patchwork, "but we did have lots of design experience,"
Mrs. Knudson stated. She has since made quilts and knows now
some of the mistakes they made in drafting the patterns. She ad-
mitted the quilts were very difficult to put together, especially the
mitered corners. "Remember we were artists! Mitered corners were
to be expected because we framed our work. We were very fussy, and
time and labor were abundant." She mentioned that one woman became so skilled at making mitered corners that she did all of them.[21]

When asked to comment about the fabric in the quilt, Mrs. Rice
said that the project wanted the very best materials available for the
quilts—for esthetic purposes and for durability. They bought very
fine color-fast percale (200 thread count) in a broad range of colors.
She said, "It was like having a palette of colors."[22] The staff developed original designs and took much time to construct them in such
a way that the quilts would be durable and would brighten the lives
of youngsters for a long time.

Fifteen different quilts are listed in the material cost list of July 5,
1939, each with a choice of colors. Three sizes were available:
Nursery Size (40 x 60 inches) for $1.25, 3/4 Size (60 x 90 inches) for
$2.45 and Full Size (80 x 90 inches) for $3.25. The pattern names

Fig. 5. Project participant quilting a Tree quilt. Courtesy Milwaukee County Museum.

are: Circles, Cherry Tree, Westover, Tulip Flower, Formal Stripe, Children's Hour, Holiday, Horse, Duck, Little Deer, Double Tree, Tree Border, Circle Border, Sailboat and Dykstra. The material cost list gives a description of each quilt pattern.[23]

Two other completed quilts have been found—one in the Milwaukee Public Museum and another in the Indianapolis Museum of Art. The one in the Milwaukee Public Museum has an original design of cabins nestled among mountain tops; it is quilted and has batting. It was not one listed in the July 5, 1939 material cost list. The stitching is not as fine as the Sailboat quilt. The Cherry Tree quilt (Figure 2) in the Indianapolis Museum of Art is exactly the same size as the Sailboat quilt, has no batting, has more than one border and has much more applique on it. Small circles representing cherries are appliqued all over the central panel.

At the Milwaukee Public Museum are many blocks of quilt patterns—possibly for use as educational samples. Only one has a printed fabric. Included in the blocks are the Cherry Tree, the Sailboat, the Cabins in the Mountain Tops, a Farmer Boy, and variations on geometic patchwork patterns. According to Miss Virginia Kazda, the research assistant of the Milwaukee Handicraft Project, the blocks currently in the collection at the Milwaukee Public

Museum were originally in the Wisconsin State Historical Society collection in Madison. The blocks had been gathered together for a retrospective exhibit called "WPA + 35" held in 1970 at the University of Wisconsin in Milwaukee (formerly the Milwaukee State Teachers College). Many of the craft items made by the Milwaukee WPA Handicraft Project were assembled for the exhibit, but only two completed quilts were included. The bulk of the craft items in the collection of the Milwaukee Public Museum were in the 1970 exhibit.[24] A slide show of the 1970 exhibit with written commentary by Miss Ulbricht is also in the history section collection of the Milwaukee Public Museum.

In the photograph scrapbooks of the WPA Handicraft Project which are now in the history section collection of the Milwaukee Public Museum are views of quilts on children's beds in an orphanage (Figure 3), quilts on display in exhibits of the project (Figure 4), women stitching quilts (Figure 5) and one doll's quilt in a child's play area.

Also in the Milwaukee Public Museum are three watercolor drawings on mat board of quilt designs: one of the Cherry Tree quilt, one of a Circle Border quilt and one of the Sailboat quilt. None is signed. Julia Loomis Knudson stated that she designed the Cherry Tree and the Circle Border quilts, and she was quite sure Dorothy Phillips Haagensen (now deceased) designed the Sailboat quilt.[25]

One final question remains; where are the quilts today? Mrs. Knudson reported that hundreds of quilts were made and as many as 100 Sailboat quilts could have been made. Many were worn out or discarded when the WPA nursery schools closed. It is, however, very possible that there are some quilts in collections of museums and schools throughout the United States. Mrs. Rice said that the crafts went to all forty-eight states, and that public institutions signed co-sponsor agreements stating that they would not resell the items.

In quilt research it is rare to find a date or a signature on a quilt from which to begin a search for answers to questions about the quilt. This particular search not only provided satisfaction from finding answers to my questions about a quilt I own, but also provided me with joy in learning some of the history of a project that was successful in many ways. The search brought alive the people, the times and an attempt to alleviate a problem not unlike problems

we face today. In the brochure which accompanied the 1970 retrospective exhibit of the WPA Milwaukee Handicraft Project, Miss
Ulbricht expressed similar feelings.

> A re-showing of this period will recall the serious conditions
> of the time similar to those of today. The exhibition will
> have the possiblities of showing a present generation and
> reminding a former generation how WPA alleviated the
> stresses of those days and how this project, well-organized
> and democratically governed, gave an understanding
> toward a better society to about 5,000 individuals of every
> age, color, and creed, skilled and unskilled, who were willing
> to work, rather than to be beholden to county sub-
> sistence.[26]

Notes and References

1. Letter from Mary June Kellogg Rice, art director, December 1984.
2. Elsa Ulbricht, "The Story of the Milwaukee Handicraft Project,"
   Design, February 1944, p. 6.
3. *Ibid.*, pp. 6–7.
4. Telephone conversation with Julia Loomis Knudson, designer in the
   WPA Milwaukee Handicraft Project, August 1984.
5. Ulbricht, p. 7.
6. Letter from M.J.K. Rice, December 1984.
7. *Record of Program Operation and Accomplishments: Milwaukee Handicraft Project*, #651.313, Final State Reports, Crafts Program-
   Wisconsin, Record Group #69, National Archives Building, pp. 1–2.
8. Elsa Ulbricht, "WPA + 35" in a brochure of *An Exhibition of Some
   Products of the Milwaukee WPA Handicrafts Project 1935–1943*, p. 2.
   (#H38316A/26013 in Milwaukee Public Museum).
9. Alberta C. Redenbaugh, #651.313, Final State Reports Vol. 1, Record
   Group #69, National Archives Building.
10. Dr. Jane Betsey Welling, "Comments About the Milwaukee WPA
    Handicraft Project," *Design*, February 1944, p. 3.

11. Letter from M.J.K. Rice, December 1984.
12. *Ibid.*
13. *Ibid.*
14. *Ibid.*
15. Andy Leon Harney, "WPA Handicrafts Rediscovered," *Historic Preservation*, July-September 1973, p. 14.
16. Gertrude Copp, "Elsa Ulbricht," *Design*, February 1944, p. 4.
17. Conversation with M.J.K. Rice, September 1984.
18. Conversation with Grace Iacolucci, student of Elsa Ulbricht, August 1984.
19. Elsa Ulbricht, letter to Mrs. Eleanor Roosevelt dated September 20, 1941. #651.313, Records of the Work Projects Administration State Correspondence, Milwaukee Handicraft Project, Records Group #69, National Archives Building.
20. WPA Handicraft Project 1170, sponsored by Milwaukee State Teachers College, p. 14. (#H32183B in Milwaukee Public Museum)
21. Conversation with Julia Loomis Knudson, August 1984.
22. Conversation M.J.K. Rice, September 1984.
23. List of Quilts and Coverlets, *Milwaukee WPA Handicraft Project Material Cost List*, #651.313, State Correspondence Files Wisconsin, Records of Work Projects Administration, Record Group #69, National Archives Building, pp. 21–24a.

Cherry Tree — Wide border design which falls to side of bed leaving inner panel of small circles (Cherries) arranged in triangular formation.

Circles — Wide border of tangent circles which fall to sides of bed leaving inner panel with striped border on top.

Westover — Very modern and simple design of squares and rectangles with row of leaves across bolster and similar design in lower right hand corner.

Tulip Flower — Tulip flowers arranged in blocks throughout whole quilt, with tulip leaf border.

Formal Stripe — Three rows of stripes (two narrow and one wide in center of each row). These alternate with four rows of leaves.

Children's Hour — Available in 40 x 60 inches size only. Large center panel of diamonds and triangles representing flowers growing out of flower pots.

Holiday — Available in 40 x 60 inches size only. Primitive design of birds and plants.

Horse — Available in 40 x 60 inches size only. Decorative horse and star alternating with plant form.

Duck—Available in 40 x 60 inches size only. One large decorative duck with simple cross design in upper left corner.

Little Deer—Available in 40 x 60 inches size only. Deer made from bias stripping alternating with plant form.

Double Tree—Inner panel double row of large and small trees, wide outer border and narrow inner panel border.

Tree Border—Border of simple triangular trees which falls to side of bed leaving inner panel with striped border on top.

Circle Border—Various widths of stripes going around four sides of quilts with applique circles in one row of stripes.

Sailboat (Child Quilt)—Pieced blocks of sailboat alternating with plain colored blocks which have a sailboat quilted on it.

Dykstra—Central leaf pattern quilted in contrasting thread.

24. Conversation with Virginia Kazda, research assistant of Milwaukee WPA Handicraft Project, September 1984.
25. Conversation with Julia Loomis Knudson, August 1984.
26. Ulbricht, "WPA + 35," p. 2.
27. Acknowledgements: Special thanks to Carter Houck for locating quilts from the Milwaukee WPA Handicraft Project, to Cuesta Benberry for sharing her materials on quilts in the WPA projects across the United States, to Mary June Kellogg Rice for her support and suggestions in compiling the information for the paper, and to the staff of the Milwaukee Public Museum for their efforts to keep the materials of the Milwaukee WPA Handicraft Project intact and available for research by the public.

INDEX

Page numbers in **boldface** refer to illustrations.

The American Quilt Study Group is a nonprofit organization devoted to the finding and dissemination of the history of quiltmaking as a significant art of women. AQSG encourages and supports research into the history of quilts, quiltmaking, quiltmakers and the textiles and materials of quilts. Membership and participation are open to all interested persons. For further information, send to the American Quilt Study Group, 105 Molino Avenue, Mill Valley, CA 94941.